10637744

Strength AND DIGNITY

A DEVOTIONAL FOR WOMEN

SHERBRINA AND TIMOTHY JONES, LEAD EDITORS

SHAMEKA AND ANTONIO DIXON, EDITORS

TIFFANY AND MAURICE WHITE, EDITORS

FORWARD PRESS
SHREVEPORT, LOUISIANA

Copyright © 2022 Forward Press

All rights reserved. No part of this publication may be reproduced, distributed, or transmitted in any form or by any means, without prior written permission.

Unless otherwise noted, Scripture quotations are taken from the New King James Version®. Copyright © 1982 by Thomas Nelson, Inc. Used by permission. All rights reserved.

Scripture quotations marked (AMP) are taken from the Amplified® Bible (AMP), Copyright © 2015 by The Lockman Foundation. Used by permission. www.Lockman.org

Scripture quotations marked (CSB) are taken from The Christian Standard Bible. Copyright © 2017 by Holman Bible Publishers. Used by permission. Christian Standard Bible®, and CSB® are federally registered trademarks of Holman Bible Publishers, all rights reserved.

Scripture quotations marked (ESV) are from The Holy Bible, English Standard Version® (ESV®), copyright © 2001 by Crossway, a publishing ministry of Good News Publishers. Used by permission. All rights reserved.

Scripture quotations marked (HCSB) are taken from the Holman Christian Standard Bible®, Copyright © 1999, 2000, 2002, 2003, 2009 by Holman Bible Publishers. Used by permission. Holman Christian Standard Bible®, Holman CSB®, and HCSB® are federally registered trademarks of Holman Bible Publishers.

Quotations marked KJV are from the King James or Authorized Version of the Bible.

Scripture quotations marked (MSG) are taken from Holy Bible: The Message (the Bible in contemporary language). 2005. Colorado Springs, CO: NavPress.

Scripture quotations marked (NIV) are taken from THE HOLY BIBLE, NEW INTERNATIONAL VERSION®, NIV® Copyright © 1973, 1978, 1984, 2011 by Biblica, Inc.™ Used by permission. All rights reserved worldwide.

Scripture quotations marked (NLT) are taken from the Holy Bible, New Living Translation, copyright © 1996, 2004, 2007 by Tyndale House Foundation. Used by permission of Tyndale House Publishers, Inc., Carol Stream, IL 60188. All rights reserved.

Scripture quotations marked (NRSV) are from the New Revised Standard Version Bible, copyright © 1989 the Division of Christian Education of the National Council of the Churches of Christ in the United States of America. Used by permission. All rights reserved.

*If there is a book that you want to read,
but it hasn't been written yet, then write it.*

TONI MORRISON

STRENGTH AND DIGNITY

FOREWORD

What am I going to wear? is a question that we ask ourselves as we ponder our activities. Some days we change our attire several times as we go from exercising, to Zoom meetings, to in-person meetings, to church, to a formal occasion, to loungewear to sleepwear. I was excited that the requested attire to a recent wedding was semi-formal. After wearing mostly casual clothes during the pandemic it felt great to be wearing dressy clothes.

I am grateful for this sisterhood of pastors' wives from different walks of life for sharing from their hearts to our hearts the importance of being dressed from the inside out.

> Do not let your adornment be merely outward—arranging the hair, wearing gold, or putting on fine apparel—rather let it be the hidden person of the heart … which is very precious in the sight of God. (1 Peter 3:3)

As you consider your daily priorities, this compilation of devotions will help you focus on your fundamental attire as prescribed by the woman in Proverbs 31:25—"Strength and honor are her clothing. She shall rejoice in time to come."

The virtuous woman in the book of Proverbs is the paragon of virtue, with noble aspirations, and wise and kind conversations. She has strength of mind and courage. She appears to be a super woman, super wife, super mother, and super planner, always looking prim and proper, causing many women to feel intimidated by her.

God wants us to appreciate the strength that He provides without becoming self-absorbed. We must dedicate our strengths to His service, being confident in Him and not ourselves. In times of stress, fatigue, and weakness we can depend upon the Lord to renew our strength. He is a promise keeper and "gives strength to the weary and increases the power of the weak. ... Those who hope in the Lord will renew their strength" (Isaiah 40:29–31 NIV).

Honor was also her clothing. She was a woman of integrity, telling the truth and keeping her promises. Thus, she was respected and had a reputation for respecting others. Some people inherit an honorable pedigree because of their family's name or accomplishments. However, she was a woman of honor because she honored God and had an industrious life serving others. God honors those who honor Him.

We must conduct ourselves honorably among people who do not know God. Proverbs 22:1 says, "A good name is to be chosen rather than great riches, loving favor rather than silver and gold." God gave her honor and she lived honorably so that God would receive the glory as she loved and served her family and community. She put others first. "She shall rejoice" in times to come because her confidence is in God who gives her fortitude of mind and the courage to stand in Him as she endures trials and trouble.

In the words of the renowned author Jill Briscoe as she penned the classic book *Queen of Hearts*, the woman in Proverbs 31 is:

> Queen of her own heart
> Queen of her husband's heart
> Queen of her children's heart
> Queen of the servant's heart
> Queen of the Lord's heart

May we emulate this woman and not be intimidated by her.

Dr. Sheila Bailey
Sheila Bailey Ministries
Dallas, Texas

Acknowledgments

We are indeed grateful for the pastors' wives who contributed to this work, as well as the support of their husbands. This work is proof that we are better together. We are also thankful for our editors: Shameka and Antonio Dixon, Sherbrina and Timothy Jones, and Tiffany and Maurice White. The technical support of Shelia Brown, O. Christopher Buckner, Sherra Crawford, Emma Shepard, and Lakisha Taylor has been remarkable. Without this phenomenal team, this project would not have been possible.

Much love and many thanks!

HOW TO USE THIS DEVOTIONAL

Draw near to God and He will draw near to you.

JAMES 4:8

Devotionals are simple, concise words of encouragement written to connect Scripture to real-life experiences and needs. Each day in this forty-day journey has an inspirational thought, Scripture readings, study questions for reflection, and a biblical promise.

1 Thessalonians 5:11 (NIV) says, "Encourage one another and build each other up." Participants are asked to create an "Encouragement Hit List" of forty people and touch one life per day. Readers should also list three things daily for which they are grateful. Research shows a significant correlation between gratitude and happiness.

Re-gifting occurs when we pass gifts that we have received along to others as gifts. The idea of "ME-gifting" is treating oneself. Participants are encouraged to "ME-gift" themselves for forty days straight but without spending any money. The goal is to practice self-care and to bless oneself with things that money cannot buy.

To maximize the experience, readers should set aside about an hour each day. It would be helpful to select an accountability partner or to invite friends to join you. This would foster connection, accountability, and encouragement. Finally, the daily declaration should be recited.

A PROVERBS 31 DECLARATION

I am a virtuous woman, and my worth is far above that of rubies. I will do good and not evil all the days of my life. I will extend my hand to those in need. I am clothed with strength and dignity. I will speak words of wisdom and kindness. I will fear the Lord and my deeds will speak for me.

PROVERBS 31:10, 12, 20, 25, 26, 30, AND 31

My Encouragement Hit List

1. _____

2. _____

3. _____

4. _____

5. _____

6. _____

7. _____

8. _____

9. _____

10. _____

11. _____

12. _____

13. _____

14. _____

15. _____

16. _____

17. _____

18. _____

19. _____

20. _____

21. _____

22. _____

23. _____

24. _____

25. _____

26. _____

27. _____

28. _____

29. _____

30. _____

31. _____

32. _____

33. _____

34. _____

35. _____

36. _____

37. _____

38. _____

39. _____

40. _____

LOVE IS REMEMBERING

Norma J. Blake

(1938–2018)

Norma J. Blake was married to the late Reverend Dr. Harry Blake for nearly sixty years. They served Mount Canaan Baptist Church in Shreveport, Louisiana for fifty-two years. Mrs. Blake was the epitome of a servant and a pastor's wife.

Renee M. White

(1975–2022)

Renee M. White was married to the Reverend Claude L. White, Jr., pastor of Grace Baptist Church in Peoria, Illinois. Renee made a posthumous contribution to this literary work. She demonstrated strength and dignity in life and death.

Forever in our hearts.

Day 1

EVEN NOW

SHERBRINA T. JONES

*"Lord," Martha said to Jesus, "if you had been here,
my brother would not have died. But I know that
even now God will give you whatever you ask."*

JOHN 11:21–22 NIV

Have you ever been disappointed with God or felt like your prayers were being ignored? There is value even in those periods of uncertainty. Alice Walker said, "Healing begins where the wound was made."

Lazarus died and Jesus was not there. Jesus was a friend of the family but absent when they needed him most. In fact, verse 5 in this chapter says, "Jesus loved Martha and her sister and Lazarus." Jesus had healed others but was in no hurry to get to Lazarus.

Both Martha and Mary said to Jesus, "If you had been here, our brother would not have died." However, Martha's faith exceeded her frustration—"But I know that even now God will give you whatever you ask."

What's really going on here? This story is bigger than Mary, Martha, and Lazarus. In verse 4, Jesus said, "This sickness will not end in death. No, it is for God's glory so that God's Son may be glorified through it."

Like Martha, many women have had "even now" moments—times when we had to find a way to trust in God, when it seemed like all hope was lost. Whether it was the death of a loved one, an unfavorable medical diagnosis, a pink slip on the job, an eviction notice, a wayward child, or a depressed spirit, we have all been there!

When I am going through one of these moments, I always ask God to reveal lessons to be learned and how He will be glorified. In the lowest places of my life, God heard my plea:

> The righteous cry out, and the LORD hears them; he delivers them from all their troubles. The LORD is close to the brokenhearted and saves those who are crushed in spirit. (Psalm 34:17–18 NIV)

I've learned that God responds in His time (and not ours!)—"At the right time, I, the LORD, will make it happen" (Isaiah 60:22 NLT). When we cannot hear or feel God, Romans 8:28 assures us that God is working for our good.

> The one thing that we can always do is believe, which is more than enough!

Martha teaches us what it means to trust God through a crisis. Martha knew Jesus as a friend; this crisis revealed Him as the Messiah. Martha went from believing that He could to seeing that He would.

> Don't just believe in miracles, expect them!

When Jesus arrived at the tomb of Lazarus he said, "Take away the stone." As Martha was blinded by the circumstances, Jesus reminded her that the key to seeing the glory of God is simply believing.

> All things are possible for one who believes. (Mark 9:23 ESV)

Perhaps Jesus is saying to us what He said to Martha: "Take away the stone!" While there are stones of despair, anxiety and fear, the biggest stone may be doubt. Toni Morrison said, "If you want to fly, you have to get rid of the thing that weighs you down." Let's remove the stones that prevent our miracles!

THOUGHT FOR TODAY

Turn your doubts into questions.
Turn your questions into prayers.
Turn your prayers to God.

MARK LITTLETON

SCRIPTURE READING

Isaiah 26:3–4

Jeremiah 32:27

1 Peter 5:7

REFLECT

1. Have you ever found it hard to truly trust God in difficult situations?

2. Are there any "stones" in your life that stand in the way of your anticipated miracle? If so, list them.

5. How has God shown that He is trustworthy?

TODAY'S PROMISE: STRENGTH

So do not fear, for I am with you; do not be dismayed, for I am your God. I will strengthen you and help you; I will uphold you with my righteous right hand.

ISAIAH 41:10 NIV

PRAYER

Dear Lord, our souls wait for You. May Your
steadfast love, O Lord, be upon us even as we
hope in You! Amen. (Psalm 33:20–22)

ENCOURAGEMENT

Who will/did you encourage today? How?

GRATITUDE

Identify three things that you are thankful for.

1.

2.

3.

ME-GIFTING

How will/did you treat yourself today?
Remember the rule: You cannot spend any money!

MY DAILY PROVERBS 31 DECLARATION

I am a virtuous woman, and my worth is far above that
of rubies. I will do good and not evil all the days of my
life. I will extend my hand to those in need. I am clothed
with strength and dignity. I will speak words of wisdom and
kindness. I will fear the Lord and my deeds will speak for me.

Proverbs 31:10, 12, 20, 25, 26, 30, and 31

Day 2

BEAUTY IS IN THE EYE OF THE BEHOLDER

MARGINA E. STAFFORD

*Let your beauty not be external—the braiding of hair
and wearing of gold jewelry or fine clothes—but the
inner person of the heart, the lasting beauty of a gentle
and tranquil spirit, which is precious in God's sight.*

I PETER 3:3–4 NET

"Magic mirror on the wall, who is the fairest one of all?"
This famous phrase from the Disney fairytale *Snow White* depicts an evil queen who is so consumed with her physical beauty that she must constantly be reassured she is the fairest in the land. What factors determine the definition of beauty?

I recently watched a series featuring Marilyn Monroe as one of the most beautiful women of all time. Her physical attributes, her mannerisms, and her style of dress were emulated by women during that era. Society established a standard of what it meant to be beautiful, and women from all over the country tried to meet those standards.

The unnerving reality is that society is constantly defining and redefining the concept of beauty. Everything from hairstyles, methods of applying makeup, nail designs, clothing and shoes change from one moment to the next. I remember buying a pair of black, pointed-toe leather boots for the winter. By the time I pulled those same boots out the next winter, one of my cousins politely shared with me that my boots were out of style and the round-toe boots were trending. The pressure to fit into these social constructs can be overwhelming and stressful. Yet, we spend time, money, and energy investing in our outward appearance out of a desire to be appealing and attractive to those we encounter.

The phrase "beauty is in the eye of the beholder" suggests that everyone has their own, subjective perspective of what beauty is. What is considered beautiful for one person may not be the case for the next. As godly women, we ought to concern ourselves primarily with the viewpoint of our Creator.

Peter writes to encourage Christian women to focus on enhancing the inner beauty of the heart. This is not to say we should neglect our outward appearance, however; his assertion is that more effort and energy should be exerted in assuring that we are beautiful from within. He further explains that inner beauty is lasting and valuable in the sight of God. Even the Lord said to Samuel:

> God does not view things the way men do. People look on the outward appearance, but the Lord looks at the heart. (1 Samuel 16:7b NET)

You cannot physically see a woman's inner beauty, but in her presence you can experience it! Some of the qualities that enhance a woman's inner beauty are a gentle and tranquil spirit, wise speech and actions, encouraging other women to behave in a godly manner, taking care of her household, giving to those who are in need, and operating in love and obedience to God.

> Charm is deceptive, and beauty does not last; but a woman who fears the Lord will be greatly praised. (Proverbs 31:30 NLT)

There will come a time where our outward beauty will begin to fade. As we age gracefully, we may develop wrinkles, fine lines, and other signs of maturing, but our inner beauty will never fade. What a blessed assurance it is to know that God will not judge our outward appearance, but His concern is with matters of our heart.

> Therefore we do not despair, but even if our physical body is wearing away, our inner person is being renewed day by day. (2 Corinthians 4:16 NET)

THOUGHTS FOR TODAY

Focus on your inner beauty.
Outer beauty will draw people to you, inner
beauty will keep them in your presence.

ROBERT OVERSTREET

Outer beauty turns the head, but inner beauty turns the heart.

HELEN J. RUSSELL

As water reflects the face, so the heart reflects the person.

PROVERBS 27:19 HCSB

SCRIPTURE READING

Proverbs 31:30

Psalm 139:14

Proverbs 3:15–18

REFLECT

1. Do you spend more effort and energy investing in your outer beauty as opposed to your inner beauty?

2. Are you more concerned about being appealing in the sight of God or the sight of man?

3. What are some inner-beauty qualities that you currently possess?

4. How can you work on enhancing your inner beauty?

TODAY'S PROMISE: PEACE

You will keep in perfect peace those whose minds are steadfast, because they trust in you.

ISAIAH 26:3 NIV

PRAYER

Father, thank You for showing me the importance of possessing inner beauty. Help me to work daily on enhancing those qualities so that I will be pleasing to You and a blessing to others. Amen.

ENCOURAGEMENT

Who will/did you encourage today? How?

GRATITUDE

Identify three things that you are thankful for.

1.

2.

3.

ME-GIFTING

How will/did you treat yourself today?
Remember the rule: You cannot spend any money!

MY DAILY PROVERBS 31 DECLARATION

I am a virtuous woman, and my worth is far above that of rubies. I will do good and not evil all the days of my life. I will extend my hand to those in need. I am clothed with strength and dignity. I will speak words of wisdom and kindness. I will fear the Lord and my deeds will speak for me.

PROVERBS 31:10, 12, 20, 25, 26, 30, AND 31

Day 3

SELF-CARE IS NOT SELFISH

SHAMEKA DIXON

He said to him, "'You shall love the Lord your God with
all your heart, and with all your soul, and with all your
mind.' This is the great and first commandment. And a
second is like it: 'You shall love your neighbor as yourself.'"

MATTHEW 22:37–39 NRSV

You deserve the love you so freely give to others. But how can you do that if you don't exhibit love for self? The term self-care was coined in the 1950s and made popular in the 1960s by the Black Panther Party. Activist Ericka Huggins encouraged self-care through practicing meditation and yoga. Find peace in knowing that you deserve your love and affection.

Self-care is a term used often, yet many of us struggle to care for our mind, body, and spirit. As women who wear many hats, we do a lot to take care of others, but we are seldom on that list. In doing that we can lose sight of self. This often can lead to mental health issues, including depression and anxiety. Let's adopt the proper perspective about self-care. Self-care is the practice of taking action to preserve or improve one's own (holistic) health. Wouldn't we be taking care of God's temple if we made time for self-care? 1 Corinthians 6:19 tells us our bodies are temples that should be cared for in honor of the God who created us.

If we are not at our best, we cannot operate in the excellence God commands from us (Colossians 3:23). Furthermore, we cannot be our best for those who depend on us. Loving others requires knowing how to love yourself. Jesus said, "You shall love the Lord your God with all your heart, and with all your soul, and with all your mind. This is the great and first commandment. And a second is like it: You shall love your neighbor as yourself."

Thus, it is important to cultivate love of self through self-care to maintain a healthy mind. There are several ways to incorporate self-care practices into your daily life. Start a gratitude journal, take a nap, or treat yourself to your favorite meal. These are ways to focus on you.

Jesus was a man who was busy taking care of the physical and spiritual needs of others. There was always someone in need of Jesus. Along his journey, Jesus stopped to be restored and encouraged his disciples to do the same. Jesus even invited his disciples to get by themselves and rest. Jesus understood the value of spending time alone to restore oneself, which often included time for praying and being refreshed by the word of God.

In all of us there is an innate desire to be loved. No matter how many times we are knocked down, let down and hurt by those we've expressed love to, we eventually give love and people another chance. This is because we were made to love, not just others, but ourselves as well. Properly loving others requires knowing how to care for oneself. Self-care is not selfish but necessary.

THOUGHTS FOR TODAY

Caring for myself is not self-indulgence, it is self-preservation, and that is an act of political warfare.

AUDRE LORDE

*Even if it makes others uncomfortable,
I will love who I am.*

JANELLE MONÁE

SCRIPTURE READING

1 Corinthians 3:16

Ephesians 2:10

Romans 8:28

1 Corinthians 10:31

Proverbs 19:21

REFLECT

1. What changes can you make to include self-care as part of your regular routine?

2. Are you able to identify your signs of stress and anxiety?

3. Who can you talk to when life gets overwhelming?

TODAY'S PROMISE: LOVE

You are loved. "But God shows his love for us in that while we were still sinners, Christ died for us"

ROMANS 5:8 ESV

PRAYER

Dear God, we know mental health is an important part
of our total health. Help us as women make taking
care of ourselves as important to us as caring for others.
When we are burdened down, let us remember You are
a heavy-load bearer. Let us be mindful of when we need
restoration. Thank You for showing what love is so we may
be better able to love others as we love ourselves. Amen.

ENCOURAGEMENT

Who will/did you encourage today? How?

GRATITUDE

Identify three things that you are thankful for.

1.

2.

3.

ME-GIFTING

How will/did you treat yourself today?
Remember the rule: You cannot spend any money!

MY DAILY PROVERBS 31 DECLARATION

I am a virtuous woman, and my worth is far above that of rubies. I will do good and not evil all the days of my life. I will extend my hand to those in need. I am clothed with strength and dignity. I will speak words of wisdom and kindness. I will fear the Lord and my deeds will speak for me.

PROVERBS 31:10, 12, 20, 25, 26, 30, AND 31

GODLY WOMEN TAKING A STAND IN AN UNGODLY WORLD

TIFFANY WHITE

Who knows if perhaps you were made
queen for just such a time as this?

ESTHER 4:14 NLT

We cannot live our lives by our own timetable, but we must learn to live according to God's divine timetable. In the Gospels, Jesus reveals to us that in life there will be seasons when it is your hour and seasons when it is not your hour to do certain things. In the Old Testament book names for her, it was Esther's hour to be used by God to deliver the people of Israel in one of their darkest hours.

When we examine the state of our communities, we see that it is time for godly women to take a stand in this ungodly world in which we live. We can no longer remain silent to the racism, economic inequality, poverty, discrimination, and crime that plague our communities. Like Esther, God has placed us here for such a time as this. How do we take a stand as godly women in an ungodly world?

The ungodliness of the culture is seen through the murderous, unrighteousness of Haman in the story of Esther. Yet, we have Esther who stands in direct contrast to Haman. Esther was actually born with the Hebrew name Hadassah, which means "myrtle." The myrtle tree is known for the pleasant aroma with which it permeates the air.

Hadassah also means "righteousness." When we are planted, rooted, and grounded in the word of God, the pleasant aroma of righteousness will fill our lives. This type of righteousness can only be achieved through our Lord and Savior Jesus Christ.

It has been said, "Action is the antidote to despair." Esther moved into action to keep the evil plot of Haman from becoming a reality. Just like Esther, we must move into action. That takes faith! God uniquely gifts each of us with abilities to carry out His plans on earth. It's no accident that we are where we are, and we've gone through what we've gone through in life. Fear not! God has prepared you for such a time as this.

THOUGHT FOR TODAY

Every great dream begins with a dreamer.
Always remember, you have within you the strength,
the patience, and the passion to reach
for the stars to change the world.

Harriet Tubman

SCRIPTURE READING

Hebrews 10:23

Philippians 1:6

1 Corinthians 15:58

1 Peter 5:9

REFLECT

1. How can you move into action to alleviate despair in your community?

2. In what ways can you exemplify Christ every day of your life?

3. Where has God placed you to be used for such a time as this?

TODAY'S PROMISE: GUIDANCE

The LORD himself goes before you and will be with you; he will never leave you nor forsake you. Do not be afraid; do not be discouraged.

DEUTERONOMY 31:8

PRAYER

Oh Lord, help me to be ready to move when Your Holy Spirit reveals opportunities to be used by You. Remove all fear and doubt so I can be used for such a time as this. In Jesus' name, amen!

ENCOURAGEMENT

Who will/did you encourage today? How?

GRATITUDE

Identify three things that you are thankful for.

1.

2.

3.

ME-GIFTING

How will/did you treat yourself today?
Remember the rule: You cannot spend any money!

MY DAILY PROVERBS 31 DECLARATION

I am a virtuous woman, and my worth is far above that of rubies. I will do good and not evil all the days of my life. I will extend my hand to those in need. I am clothed with strength and dignity. I will speak words of wisdom and kindness. I will fear the Lord and my deeds will speak for me.

PROVERBS 31:10, 12, 20, 25, 26, 30, AND 31

Day 5

WHO ARE YOU?

LOIS THOMAS

*The dogs shall eat Jezebel on the plot of ground at
Jezreel, and there shall be none to bury her.*

2 KINGS 9:10

*Who can find a virtuous wife?
For her worth is far above rubies.*

PROVERBS 31:10

No one wants to be known as an untruthful person, a murderer, or a coveter. The Ten Commandments emphatically condemn such behavior, yet Jezebel was all of the above. In fact, she even practiced idolatry. No wonder we do not name our daughters Jezebel!

At some point in life, we must look in the mirror and ask, "Who are you?" We should also ask, "What do you want to be?" While no decent woman wants to be a Jezebel, it takes much effort to be a Proverbs 31 woman.

Psalm 1 does a perfect job of contrasting the lives of the faithful and the unfaithful. The faithful—happy or blessed—person does not follow the advice of the ungodly or join in the activities of sinners. They find joy in the law of the Lord; thus, they are planted, productive, and prosperous! Faithless, ungodly people are like worthless chaff, scattered in the wind. Their ultimate fate is sealed. They will be condemned at the time of judgment.

The Proverbs 31 woman is everything that Jezebel was not. Jezebel was evil; the Proverbs 31 woman is virtuous. Jezebel worshiped idols; the Proverbs 31 woman "fears the Lord."

Jezebel took the lives of innocent people. Though we have not literally stoned other people, 1 John 3:15 says, "Everyone who hates his brother is a murderer." Like guns, the tongue is lethal. James 3:8 says it is "full of deadly poison."

> With his mouth the godless man would destroy his neighbor. (Proverbs 11:9 ESV)

> Death and life are in the power of the tongue. (Proverbs 18:21 ESV)

The virtuous woman in Proverbs 31 is trustworthy. She is loving, caring, and kind. She is a blessing to her family and anyone in need. She is industrious, not idle. It's been said that idle hands are the devil's tools. The virtuous woman even sets an example for our speech:

> She opens her mouth with wisdom, And on her tongue *is* the law of kindness. (Proverbs 31:26)

Let's walk in our value as women of God. May our families and friends see God reflected in our character. We are virtuous women and our worth is "far above that of rubies." By the way, Jezebel is NOT the woman any of us would want to be. She literally went to the dogs!

THOUGHT FOR TODAY

You do not need to be perfect,
just be better than you were yesterday.

AUTHOR UNKNOWN

SCRIPTURE READING

Psalm 1

Colossians 3:5

Philippians 4:8–9

REFLECT
---

1. Have I injured someone today?

2. Am I pleasing God with my life?

3. Am I making right choices?

4. Is my life helping someone today?

TODAY'S PROMISE: COMFORT

Come to me, all you who are weary and burdened, and I will give you rest. Take my yoke upon you and learn from me, for I am gentle and humble in heart, and you will find rest for your souls.

MATTHEW 11:28–29 NIV

PRAYER

Lord, touch us in a mighty way, that we will always trust in You for guidance through Your word. Help us to bless others as You bless us. Amen.

ENCOURAGEMENT

Who will/did you encourage today? How?

GRATITUDE

Identify three things that you are thankful for.

1.

2.

3.

ME-GIFTING

How will/did you treat yourself today?

Remember the rule: You cannot spend any money!

MY DAILY PROVERBS 31 DECLARATION

I am a virtuous woman, and my worth is far above that of rubies. I will do good and not evil all the days of my life. I will extend my hand to those in need. I am clothed with strength and dignity. I will speak words of wisdom and kindness. I will fear the Lord and my deeds will speak for me.

PROVERBS 31:10, 12, 20, 25, 26, 30, AND 31

Day 6

YOU ALREADY KNOW!

RAQUEL PIGEE

*And we know that all things work together for good to them that
love God, to them who are called according to his purpose.*

ROMANS 8:28 KJV

Have you ever had an "already" friend? Every time you bring up
something in conversation, this friend already knows everything
about the subject. If you say something about a good recipe, they've
already cooked it. If you share that you traveled to a wonderful place
on vacation, they've already been there. If you tell them about a new
shopping spot, their response is "Girrrrl—I already shopped there
last week."

I know you can relate to this kind of friend. It's funny, because we
may get a little upset with them, but we know that we can go to them
and get great insight, because they already know."

Gut-wrenching issues in life cause us to sometimes wonder how
things will turn out for us. Fortunately, as women who love the Lord
and are called according to His purpose, we already know that things
will work together for our good. This fact is extremely comforting as we
face challenges. Regardless of feeling discouraged at times, we already
know that it's going to work out for our good.

You already know! My sister, your trials will turn around in your
favor. The storm that you thought would destroy you worked out to
deliver you. Now you are stronger than you have ever been. That lesson

that you bought was quite expensive. The growth that you have experienced since that season in your life is priceless. Yep, it all worked out for your good. Look up! Move on! It hurt you, but you can't allow it to hinder you. Take off that heavy backpack of unforgiveness and free yourself! It's working out for your good. You already know!

Hold your head up, Sis! Smile. God is in control. In Romans 8:1 (KJV) Paul encourages us to be confident in our walk with Christ and that we are eternally secure: "There is therefore now no condemnation to them which are in Christ Jesus, who walk not after the flesh, but after the Spirit."

"If God be for us, who can be against us?" (Romans 8:31 KJV)

Rest assured, it may seem messy, but it's going to turn out marvelous. You already know that things will work out for your good when you love the Lord and are called according to His purpose.

THOUGHT FOR TODAY

Challenges make you discover things about yourself you never really knew. They're what makes the instrument stretch, what makes you go beyond the norm.

CICELY TYSON

SCRIPTURE READING

Psalm 118:6–9

Isaiah 40:31

Isaiah 41:10

Philippians 4:13

REFLECT

1. What has God delivered you from that you thought you would not get through?

2. Name behaviors or actions that reflect a woman who loves the Lord and has been called according to His purpose.

3. What are some ways to focus on who you are in Christ and not on negativity?

TODAY'S PROMISE: GRACE

But he said to me, "My grace is sufficient for you, for my power is made perfect in weakness." Therefore, I will boast all the more gladly about my weaknesses, so that Christ's power may rest on me. That is why, for Christ's sake, I delight in weaknesses, in insults, in hardships, in persecutions, in difficulties. For when I am weak, then I am strong.

2 Corinthians 12:9–10 niv

PRAYER

Dear Lord, thank You for the promise that all things will work for our good when we love You and are called according to Your purpose. Please help us to focus on our power in You and not on what we may be feeling during times of struggle. Strengthen us and please bring Your word to our remembrance so that we will remain confident. Amen.

ENCOURAGEMENT

Who will/did you encourage today? How?

GRATITUDE

Identify three things that you are thankful for.

1.

2.

3.

ME-GIFTING

How will/did you treat yourself today?
Remember the rule: You cannot spend any money!

MY DAILY PROVERBS 31 DECLARATION

I am a virtuous woman, and my worth is far above that of rubies. I will do good and not evil all the days of my life. I will extend my hand to those in need. I am clothed with strength and dignity. I will speak words of wisdom and kindness. I will fear the Lord and my deeds will speak for me.

PROVERBS 31:10, 12, 20, 25, 26, 30, AND 31

AND SHE LIVED HAPPILY EVER AFTER

TANECA DENNIS

Boaz asked the overseer of his harvesters,
"Who does that young woman belong to?"

RUTH 2:5 NIV

So Boaz took Ruth, and she became his wife. And he
went in to her, and the LORD gave her conception, and
she bore a son. Then the women said to Naomi, "Blessed
be the LORD, who has not left you this day without a
redeemer, and may his name be renowned in Israel!"

RUTH 4:13–14 ESV

The story of Cinderella is the story of a meek, good girl that lost her mother. Her father married another woman. Unfortunately, the stepmother was a real example of an evil stepmother. She made Cinderella do all the hard work around the house. Although Cinderella was diligent and kept trying to be good with her new mother and her daughters, they refused her. Despite her position, chores, and the place where she was forced to reside, poor Cinderella was still the most beautiful among the daughters.

Cinderella had a fairy godmother who helped make her wishes come true. She won the prince with her beauty but remained modest and humble. She didn't hold a grudge and didn't take revenge on her stepsisters, even when she had a chance. When they asked for forgiveness, she was gracious and forgave them for everything they'd done to her. That way she could enjoy life with her prince and live happily ever after.

To some degree, Cinderella sounds like Ruth. Ruth was a young woman who escaped a life of reproach and poverty by meeting a wealthy prince. He swept Ruth off her feet and made her his bride. The difference between Ruth and Cinderella is that the book of Ruth is no fairytale—no pumpkins turn into carriages. This is a real-life story set amidst the hardships of everyday circumstances. The miraculous occurrences that unfold were arranged by God the heavenly Father, not by a fairy godmother.

Ruth teaches us that God has a bigger plan and purpose for our lives. Can we be honest? Some days we look in the mirror and don't see the image and likeness of God. We see women who are flawed and failing.

But in Matthew 10:31 (ESV), Jesus says, "Fear not, therefore; you are of more value than many sparrows." And in Jeremiah 31:3, the Lord says, "Yes, I have loved you with an everlasting love; therefore with lovingkindness I have drawn you."

God sometimes puts us in uncomfortable situations where the process is painful and hard, but where we will grow and He will get the glory. I Corinthians 2:9 (KJV) says, "But as it is written, Eye hath not seen, nor ear heard, neither have entered into the heart of man, the things which God hath prepared for them that love him."

God has made us remarkable women. Whether single or married, we have value. We are students and homemakers. We are attorneys and doctors. We are executives and even a vice president of the United States.

Just like stars can't shine without darkness, we shine best in dark times. When we consider the stories of Cinderella and Ruth, then consider your own story. Stay devoted, diligent, and dutiful, and you too can "live happily ever after."

THOUGHTS FOR TODAY

A strong woman knows she has strength enough for the journey, but a woman of strength knows it is in the journey where she will become strong.

AUTHOR UNKNOWN

We may encounter many defeats, but we must not be defeated.

MAYA ANGELOU

SCRIPTURE READING

Ruth 3:11

Proverbs 22:1

REFLECT

1. How would you evaluate your attitude toward humility and submission?

2. Do you have qualities similar to Cinderella? How about Ruth? If so, please explain.

3. If you could have a right-now, present-day conversation with Ruth, what encouragement would you give her about life?

TODAY'S PROMISE: HOPE

But those who hope in the LORD will renew their strength. They will soar on wings like eagles; they will run and not grow weary, they will walk and not be faint.

ISAIAH 40:31 NIV

PRAYER

Dear Lord, help me to be faithful, diligent and strong. I will allow Your word to dwell in me so that I may go forth with the promises and plans that You have for my life. Amen.

ENCOURAGEMENT

Who will/did you encourage today? How?

GRATITUDE

Identify three things that you are thankful for.

1.

2.

3.

ME-GIFTING

How will/did you treat yourself today?

Remember the rule: You cannot spend any money!

MY DAILY PROVERBS 31 DECLARATION

I am a virtuous woman, and my worth is far above that of rubies. I will do good and not evil all the days of my life. I will extend my hand to those in need. I am clothed with strength and dignity. I will speak words of wisdom and kindness. I will fear the Lord and my deeds will speak for me.

PROVERBS 31:10, 12, 20, 25, 26, 30, AND 31

Day 1

THE ANSWER'S
AT THE DOOR

JUDY GREER

*"When she recognized Peter's voice, she was so overjoyed
that, instead of opening the door, she ran back inside
and told everyone, "Peter is standing at the door!"*

ACTS 12:14 NLT

Are you believing God to do what you are asking Him for in prayer? A part of answered prayer is believing what you are praying for will come to fruition. Jesus said, "Whatever you ask in prayer, believe that you have received it, and it will be yours" (Mark 11:24 RSV).

Intercession is one of the types of prayer and entails making requests to God on behalf of others. Not only does the Holy Spirit intercede on our behalf (Romans 8:26–27), but we are to intercede for each other (James 5:16).

In Acts chapter 12, Peter was in prison and was miraculously rescued by an angel. He originally thought he was seeing a vision, but when he came to his senses, he realized that what was being done by the angel was real.

Sisters, your miracle will require your participation. The angel told Peter to get up, get dressed, put on his sandals and coat, and follow him. Peter did not question the angel but obeyed the angel's orders. The answers to our prayers are directly tied to whether we obey the voice of God.

While Peter was in prison, the church gathered at Mary's house for prayer. No doubt they were praying for Peter's release. *Guess what?* While they were in prayer, Peter knocked on the door! A servant girl named Rhoda answered. She recognized his voice and was so overjoyed she forgot to open the door.

Rhoda ran back inside to let everyone know the answer to their prayers was at the door! Peter was standing at the door! The problem is they didn't believe Rhoda. They didn't believe it was Peter, but thought it was his angel. *Peter kept knocking.*

When they finally answered the door and saw him, they were amazed. Sisters, don't be amazed when the answer to your prayer knocks on the door. God has promised to meet our needs and He is faithful to perform miracles on our behalf.

There are times when we need others to pray for us. One night in 2019, I experienced a traumatic accident: I fell down the stairs in my home. The accident left me unconscious and fighting for my life for days. There were times when they thought I might not wake up, but the church prayed for healing, and healing came knocking on the door!

While the accident left some lasting effects, I am a witness and testimony that when the church prays, miracles, signs, and wonders are possible. Don't be surprised when your answer comes. God sometimes shows up unexpectantly. Expect God to do just what you are asking Him for. The answer's at the door!

THOUGHT FOR TODAY

*A part of answered prayer is believing God will
do what you are asking Him to do.*

SCRIPTURE READING

Mark 11:24

Romans 8:26–27

James 5:16

REFLECT

1. Why do you think some people find it difficult to believe God will answer their prayers?

2. Have there been times when you doubted God? What did you do to alleviate your doubt?

3. After you pray, what are your next steps?

TODAY'S PROMISE: DESTINY

"For I know the plans I have for you," declares the LORD, "plans to prosper you and not to harm you, plans to give you hope and a future."

JEREMIAH 29:11 NIV

PRAYER

Lord, teach me to pray urgently, persistently, and with clarity, expecting You to answer my prayers. In the name of Jesus, amen!

ENCOURAGEMENT

Who will/did you encourage today? How?

GRATITUDE

Identify three things that you are thankful for.

1.

2.

3.

ME-GIFTING

How will/did you treat yourself today?
Remember the rule: You cannot spend any money!

MY DAILY PROVERBS 31 DECLARATION

I am a virtuous woman, and my worth is far above that of rubies. I will do good and not evil all the days of my life. I will extend my hand to those in need. I am clothed with strength and dignity. I will speak words of wisdom and kindness. I will fear the Lord and my deeds will speak for me.

PROVERBS 31:10, 12, 20, 25, 26, 30, AND 31

Day 1

LET IT GO!

ALVESTER WILLIAMS BARFIELD

*Forbearing one another, and forgiving one another, if any man have
a quarrel against any: even as Christ forgave you, so also do ye.*

COLOSSIANS 3:13 KJV

One of the hardest things I have had to do was to forgive a person that I'd considered a trusted friend. The betrayal of this friend left such an awful and bitter feeling in my heart. This was someone with whom I'd shared and to whom I'd vented about everything in life, only to find in turn that they did not share vital information with me regarding an upcoming promotion at our shared workplace. There were underhanded, deceptive moves in play that I did not notice. My friend was not only privy to the latter, but also a part of what would result in them getting the position and me, the best candidate, being overlooked.

Yes, it took a few years and a great deal of prayer for me to reach a place of complete peace and forgiveness. Taking control of my feelings of hurt and pain meant that I would have to admit to myself that what I deemed as betrayal was God saying, "It's not yet your time, child." I did not want to accept that, and I suffered spiritually. I chose to stew in self-pity and wounded pride rather than acknowledge God's perfect timing and offer forgiveness.

Forgiveness is so crucial for the believers of Christ to have a healthy spiritual life. Jesus taught us to pray: "Forgive us our debts as we forgive our debtors." He also taught that we are to forgive others because God has already forgiven us.

The Lord gave me space and time to fully understand that forgiveness is not about me but about my relationship with Him. He patiently guided me as I quarreled within myself and with others. I now know that the forgiveness Christ gave but did not owe me is the same forgiveness I should offer all who offend me. Peter asked Jesus, "Lord, how often shall my brother sin against me, and I forgive him? Up to seven times? Jesus said to him, "I do not say to you, up to seven times, but up to seventy times seven"(Matthew 18:21–22).

What hurt are you dealing with and cannot seem to move past? Turn to God and seek Him for the healing you need so that you may be able to forgive others as He has forgiven you. As the English poet Alexander Pope said, "To err is human, to forgive, divine."

THOUGHT FOR TODAY

My mission in life is not merely to survive, but to thrive; and to do so with some passion, some compassion, some humour, and some style.

MAYA ANGELOU

SCRIPTURE READING

Mark 11:25–26

Luke 17:4

REFLECT

1. What is the benefit of forgiveness?

2. Is there someone you need to forgive? If so, what is keeping you from forgiving that person?

TODAY'S PROMISE: SERENITY

Do not be anxious about anything,
but in every situation, by prayer and petition,
with thanksgiving, present your requests to God.

Philippians 4:6 niv

PRAYER

Dear heavenly Father, thank You for forgiving me for
every sin and act of transgression. I thank You for giving
me the spirit of forgiveness that I might continue to
have communion with You and Your people. Amen

ENCOURAGEMENT

Who will/did you encourage today? How?

GRATITUDE

Identify three things that you are thankful for.

1.

2.

3.

ME-GIFTING

How will/did you treat yourself today?
Remember the rule: You cannot spend any money!

MY DAILY PROVERBS 31 DECLARATION

I am a virtuous woman, and my worth is far above that of rubies. I will do good and not evil all the days of my life. I will extend my hand to those in need. I am clothed with strength and dignity. I will speak words of wisdom and kindness. I will fear the Lord and my deeds will speak for me.

PROVERBS 31:10, 12, 20, 25, 26, 30, AND 31

CHECK YOUR CREW, BOO!

DIONDRA MCFARLAND

Be not deceived: "Bad company corrupts good morals."
1 Corinthians 15:33 hcsb

I f you attended Sunday school at all as a child, you should remember what was going on at the church at Corinth and why Paul wrote this letter to the saints there. If you have never attended Sunday school, that's okay; I'll give you a little background for context. The Corinthian church had a myriad of problems, including claims of spiritual superiority, sexual immorality, suing one another in public court, and abusing the Lord's Supper. Paul's letter demanded higher ethical and moral standards.

A woman of strength and dignity is careful of who she allows in her inner circle and who she calls a "friend." True godly friendships should encourage you to be the best version of yourself and to be a person of integrity. Godly friends should be willing to listen without judgment, and at times call you on the carpet when you're engaging in behavior that is unbecoming for a woman of God.

You should stay away from people who remind you of your past failures and indiscretions, repeat your secrets, and rehearse your vulnerabilities and insecurities. The book of Proverbs offers several warnings for those who find pleasure in discussing the sensitive areas of their lives:

> A perverse person stirs up conflict, and a gossip separates
> close friends. (Proverbs 16:28 niv)

He who covers and forgives an offense seeks love, but he who repeats or gossips about a matter separates intimate friends. (Proverbs 17:9 AMP)

When is the last time you did a "crew check"? Are the people closest to you positive? Do they influence you negatively? Do they encourage you to get involved in unhealthy, unproductive behavior?

Get you a praying crew! People you can call at midnight to pray. People who would never betray your trust or share your secrets. Surround yourself with people who walk in integrity at all times, not only when someone is looking. *Check your crew!*

Four Qualities of a Healthy Friend

1. Appeals to your faith and not your flesh. (Psalm 1:1)

2. Tells you the truth even when it's difficult to hear. (Proverbs 8:8–9)

3. Prays with and for you! Sharing your struggles with a trusted friend is liberating.

4. Encourages you to become the best that you can be. (Proverbs 27:17)

THOUGHTS FOR TODAY

You're known by the company that you keep.

AESOP

Friends are like elevators; they'll take you up or they'll bring you down.

JOHN MAXWELL

*Your environment will change you before
you change your environment.*

BISHOP I. V. HILLIARD

SCRIPTURE READING

Proverbs 17:17

Proverbs 29:7

Ecclesiastes 4:9–10

1 Thessalonians 5:11

REFLECT
---

1. Why is it important to surround yourself with friends who are righteous and walk in integrity?

2. Let's do a quick "crew check." Can you identify those friends who are walking contrary to the word of God? Are they causing you to compromise your commitment to righteousness?

3. What's your next step?

TODAY'S PROMISE: RIGHTEOUSNESS

"He himself bore our sins" in his body on the cross,
so that we might die to sins and live for righteousness;
"by his wounds you have been healed."

1 Peter 2:24 NIV

PRAYER

Jesus, help me to be able to discern who is a friend
and who is not. Send into my life those who
will not make me bitter but better. Amen!

ENCOURAGEMENT

Who will/did you encourage today? How?

GRATITUDE

Identify three things that you are thankful for.

1.

2.

3.

ME-GIFTING

How will/did you treat yourself today?
Remember the rule: You cannot spend any money!

MY DAILY PROVERBS 31 DECLARATION

I am a virtuous woman, and my worth is far above that
of rubies. I will do good and not evil all the days of my
life. I will extend my hand to those in need. I am clothed
with strength and dignity. I will speak words of wisdom and
kindness. I will fear the Lord and my deeds will speak for me.

PROVERBS 31:10, 12, 20, 25, 26, 30, AND 31

POWER OF THE TOUCH

BARBARA VAUGHT

And a certain woman, which had an issue of blood twelve years,
And had suffered many things of many physicians, and had spent
all that she had, and was nothing bettered, but rather grew worse.

MARK 5:25–26 KJV

What do you do when things get worse? The woman with the issue of blood invested all she had with hopes, dreams, expectations, and strength—only to get worse. Can you see that she was physically, mentally, emotionally, and possibly spiritually crushed? Sometimes when our resources run out, we can only act in faith. This woman decided to touch Jesus, although she knew that everything she touched would be considered unclean.

She believed the power of Jesus was stronger than the power of her plague. She chose to break the law because she needed her breakthrough. Her dilemma appeared hopeless until contact with Jesus changed her situation from doom to deliverance.

After meeting Jesus, she was no longer the same. Jesus did not identify her as the woman with the issue of blood; he called her "daughter." Jesus declared her whole and spoke peace upon her, and for the first time in twelve years, she was not required to separate herself. Perhaps we allow our issues to isolate us when our healing is in our making contact with Jesus.

I see my story in her story. Several years ago, I was diagnosed with cancer. I was consumed with it. I struggled daily, crying out to God. I tried to manage the best I could. Then one day after work I went home, laid flat on my back, lifted my hand to God, and prayed. I gave it ALL to Him. I felt the weight lifted off me, and I knew the power of God was working. As Isaiah 40:29 (NIV) says, "He gives strength to the weary and increases the power of the weak."

I realized when we trust Jesus, the only thing we have to lose is our burden. Psalm 55: 22 (KJV) says, "Cast thy burden upon the Lord, and he shall sustain thee: he shall never suffer the righteous to be moved."

Are you gripped by grief? Frozen by fear? Defeated by doubt? God can transform fear into faith, your grief into glory, and your doubts into deliverance. "Trust in the LORD with all thine heart; and lean not unto thine own understanding" (Proverbs 3:5 KJV).

As Michelle Obama once said, "You may not always have a comfortable life and you will not always be able to solve all of the world's problems at once but don't ever underestimate the importance you can have because history has shown us that courage can be contagious and hope can take on a life of its own."

THOUGHT FOR TODAY

Not all storms come to disrupt your life;
some come to clear your path.

AUTHOR UNKNOWN

SCRIPTURE READING

Deuteronomy 31:6

Leviticus 15:25–27

Mark 5:25–29

Luke 8:43–48

REFLECT

1. What is your greatest hindrance to stepping out in faith? How will you overcome it?

2. How would you use your experience to help someone through their struggle?

3. Are you familiar with the woman with the issue of blood? Can you see yourself in her?

4. How will you apply this experience to your life going forward?

TODAY'S PROMISE: PERSEVERANCE

Consider it pure joy, my brothers and sisters, whenever you face trials of many kinds, because you know that the testing of your faith produces perseverance.

James 1:2–3 niv

PRAYER

Dear Lord, give me the strength to step out in faith and expect You to deliver. I am grateful that I can come to You when I need healing of any kind. Even though I am less than worthy, thank You for accepting me regardless of me. Amen.

ENCOURAGEMENT

Who will/did you encourage today? How?

GRATITUDE

Identify three things that you are thankful for.

1.

2.

3.

ME-GIFTING

How will/did you treat yourself today?
Remember the rule: You cannot spend any money!

MY DAILY PROVERBS 31 DECLARATION

I am a virtuous woman, and my worth is far above that of rubies. I will do good and not evil all the days of my life. I will extend my hand to those in need. I am clothed with strength and dignity. I will speak words of wisdom and kindness. I will fear the Lord and my deeds will speak for me.

PROVERBS 31:10, 12, 20, 25, 26, 30, AND 31

Day 12

THE POWER OF A PRAYING WOMAN

BETTY COOPER ROSE

After they had eaten and drunk in Shiloh, Hannah rose. Now Eli the priest was sitting on the seat beside the doorpost of the temple of the LORD. She was deeply distressed and prayed to the LORD and wept bitterly. And she vowed a vow and said, "O LORD of hosts, if you will indeed look on the affliction of your servant and remember me and not forget your servant, but will give to your servant a son, then I will give him to the LORD all the days of his life, and no razor shall touch his head."

1 SAMUEL 1:9–11 ESV

In *The Power of a Praying Woman,* Stormie Omartian exclaimed, "We will never be happy until we make God the source of our fulfillment and the answer to our longing." Hannah is a classic example of the power of a praying woman. Hannah was a woman of prayer, patience, and persistence even when the odds were stacked against her.

Though barren, ridiculed by her husband's other wife, and accused of being drunk by the priest, Hannah remained faithful to God. She teaches us how to live authentic, godly lives regardless of the circumstances confronting us.

Prayer is a great source of strength when facing insurmountable problems. Hannah illustrates how faith in God brings hope in times of affliction. Hannah was clothed in strength and dignity!

And she was in bitterness of soul, and prayed unto the
LORD, and wept sore. (1 Samuel 1:10 KJV)

I can relate to Hannah's story wholeheartedly. Although our stories
are different, they are similar. I can feel Hannah's heart. Hannah did
not have a child; I lost a child. Can you imagine how devastated I was
to hear that my eighteen-year-old was given only six months to live? I
found peace in God's assurance that my child was His child.

When God answered Hannah's prayer, she did as she'd promised
and dedicated him to the Lord. Hannah gave her child to the Lord and
so did I. For Hannah, it was in delight. For me, it was in death. None-
theless, both were given for the glory of God.

In everything give thanks; for this is the will of God in
Christ Jesus for you. (1 Thessalonians 5:18)

Perhaps you have had a situation where you needed God's assis-
tance and you prayed expecting God to answer quickly, but He didn't.
Let me assure you that prayer delayed is not prayer denied.

And in due time Hannah conceived and bore a son, and
she called his name Samuel, for she said, "I have asked for
him from the Lord." (1 Samuel 1:20 ESV)

THOUGHT FOR TODAY

Great things never come from comfort zones.

AUTHOR UNKNOWN

SCRIPTURE READING

1 Thessalonians 5:17

Matthew 6:9–13

Philippians 4:6

REFLECT

1. What are you willing to give up for God's glory?

2. List three times when God answered your prayers.

3. What changes are you willing to make to become a woman of strength and dignity?

TODAY'S PROMISE: ANSWERED PRAYER

*This is the confidence we have in approaching God:
that if we ask anything according to his will, he hears
us. And if we know that he hears us—whatever we
ask—we know that we have what we asked of him.*

1 JOHN 5:14–15 NIV

PRAYER

Lord, thank You for being my provider and protector,
for every good and perfect gift comes from You. Give
me the strength to wait patiently on Your promises
and purpose for my life. In Jesus' name, amen!

ENCOURAGEMENT

Who will/did you encourage today? How?

GRATITUDE

Identify three things that you are thankful for.

1.

2.

3.

ME-GIFTING

How will/did you treat yourself today?
Remember the rule: You cannot spend any money!

MY DAILY PROVERBS 31 DECLARATION

I am a virtuous woman, and my worth is far above that of rubies. I will do good and not evil all the days of my life. I will extend my hand to those in need. I am clothed with strength and dignity. I will speak words of wisdom and kindness. I will fear the Lord and my deeds will speak for me.

PROVERBS 31:10, 12, 20, 25, 26, 30, AND 31

YOU SHALL SURVIVE!

ANNA RIDEAU-TRAMMELL

*"The Lord repay your work, and a full reward be given you by
the LORD God of Israel, under whose wings you have come for
refuge." Then she said, "Let me find favor in thy sight, my lord;
for you have comforted me, and have spoken kindly to your
maidservant, though I am not like one of your maidservants."*

RUTH 2:12–13

You may have read or heard "Ruth got her Boaz," but what we fail to realize is that Boaz got himself a RUTH! Ruth was not just any woman. She had already been chosen and written into the plan of God. As a matter of fact, Ruth wasn't even a Jew; she was grafted into the family of God just like us.

A Moabite, Ruth married into a family of Israelites. Unfortunately, her husband and all the other men of the family died. Naomi, Ruth's mother-in-law, buried her husband and her sons, leaving Ruth and Naomi in a critical situation.

Ruth and Naomi's chapter one ended with death. Yes, Naomi was upset. Yes, Naomi was hurt, and she had every right to be. But Naomi had to get up, pull herself together, and decide if she wanted to live or die. I believe Naomi realized God's promises for her life had not been buried but were waiting for her in Bethlehem, and Ruth tagged along.

Ruth followed Naomi's God, Naomi's teachings, and Naomi's instructions, and by the time we get to chapter four, we see success and life. Ruth and Naomi went from just enough to more than enough. They went from tragedy to triumph! Ruth went from a widow to a wife. She went from gleaning in the fields to owning the fields! These sisters leveled up!

Because of Ruth's faithfulness to Naomi and accepting her family and her God, Ruth was blessed! God's promises have not been buried and "trouble don't last always!" At times, unplanned or unexpected events in our lives will knock us down, but we can't let them take us out. Girlfriend, get up and level up!! Life is waiting on you!

Ruth had the counsel of one wise woman and worked only in one field. Ruth worked hard to take care of Naomi and herself, and Boaz took notice. Through Boaz, God was showing Ruth that her love and commitment to Naomi had not gone unnoticed.

Stay faithful in the field where God has you. Work your field! When necessary, seek the counsel of wise women. Don't be afraid to ask for help when help is needed. Seeking the counsel of wise women can make a difference in your destiny. See you at the top!

THOUGHT FOR TODAY

Surround yourself with only people who are going to lift you higher.

OPRAH WINFREY

SCRIPTURE READING

Revelation 2:10

Proverbs 16:3

1 Peter 5:6–7

REFLECT

1. In what ways can you be more faithful to your family and friends?

2. How has God shown you that your faithfulness is not unnoticed?

3. Who are the women in your life that can offer you wise counsel?

TODAY'S PROMISE: PROTECTION

*Surely he will save you from the fowler's snare
and from the deadly pestilence.*

PSALM 91:3 NIV

PRAYER

Lord, I want to be faithful to You even in the worst
of times. I humble myself before You, knowing that
You are able to take me to higher heights. Amen.

ENCOURAGEMENT

Who will/did you encourage today? How?

GRATITUDE

Identify three things that you are thankful for.

1.

2.

3.

ME-GIFTING

How will/did you treat yourself today?

Remember the rule: You cannot spend any money!

MY DAILY PROVERBS 31 DECLARATION

I am a virtuous woman, and my worth is far above that of rubies. I will do good and not evil all the days of my life. I will extend my hand to those in need. I am clothed with strength and dignity. I will speak words of wisdom and kindness. I will fear the Lord and my deeds will speak for me.

PROVERBS 31:10, 12, 20, 25, 26, 30, AND 31

Day 14

TAKING THOUGHTS CAPTIVE

TIFFANY JARRETT

We destroy arguments and every lofty opinion raised against the knowledge of God, and take every thought captive to obey Christ.

2 CORINTHIANS 10:5 ESV

There once was a woman from a small town that had big dreams. At the age of nineteen, she started the process of pursuing her dreams of becoming an actress. Unbeknownst to her, she would face detrimental trials and tribulations that lead to homelessness, brokenness, and major setbacks.

She continued to press and follow her dreams and to believe the plan that God had for her life. She made a promise to God that she would continue to trust and follow Him. This woman is Tabatha Brown. Tabatha is famous for her positive and encouraging self-talks. Her story is an example of how God desires us to speak to ourselves in a positive, uplifting way.

Psychology Today

According to the National Science Foundation the average person has about 12,000 to 60,000 thoughts per day. Of those, 80 percent are negative and 95 percent are the same repetitive thoughts from the day before. What about you? How many of your thoughts today reflect this statistic?

Often, we are engulfed in a cycle of negativity that becomes habit. We bash ourselves for being overweight, overspending, being an inpatient mother, being an untrusting wife, missing opportunities, being anxious, being fearful, not working out, being emotional, being overwhelmed … and the list goes on. We wake up thinking these things about ourselves and we go to bed with these things on our mind repeatedly.

What God Says

The good news is that we serve a God who understands and has given us biblical affirmations to combat these negative thoughts. Even in our tirade of feelings, know that feelings are not always facts.

In order to take thoughts captive, they must be on the forefront of your mind. Continuously be present in your thinking. Replay what you have said to yourself during the day or at any given time. If your thoughts aren't loving and positive, replace them with Scripture. For example:

> **Your thought:** "I feel like a failure."
>
> **God's Word:** Being confident of this, that he who began a good work in you will carry it on to completion until the day of Christ Jesus. (Philippians 1:6 NIV)
>
> **Your thought:** "I am always anxious; nothing can change that."
>
> **God's Word:** Cast all your anxiety on him because he cares for you. (1 Peter 5:7 NIV)
>
> **Your thought:** "I am a bad parent."
>
> **God's Word:** Her children rise up and call her blessed; her husband also, and he praises her: "Many women have done excellently, but you surpass them all." (Proverbs 31:28–29 ESV)

Nothing has more impact to shift our minds and lives than knowing who we are and the power and authority we have been given. (Jennie Allen)

THOUGHT FOR TODAY

*Take a day to heal from the lies you've told yourself
and the ones that have been told to you.*

Maya Angelou

SCRIPTURE READING

Psalm 139:14

2 Corinthians 10:7

Philippians 4:8

REFLECT

1. What thoughts are holding you captive and how are you going to combat them in the word?

2. What does God say about who we are?

3. Take a moment to reflect on the positive things about you. Write them down.

TODAY'S PROMISE: ASSURANCE

*And we know that in all things God works for the good of those
who love him, who have been called according to his purpose.*

Romans 8:28 niv

PRAYER

Dear Lord, forgive us for trusting our voices more than we trust Yours. Help us to see ourselves as the wonderful creation that You called us to be. May our lives reflect the truth of who You have said that we are. Amen.

ENCOURAGEMENT

Who will/did you encourage today? How?

GRATITUDE

Identify three things that you are thankful for.

1.

2.

3.

ME-GIFTING

How will/did you treat yourself today?

Remember the rule: You cannot spend any money!

MY DAILY PROVERBS 31 DECLARATION

I am a virtuous woman, and my worth is far above that of rubies. I will do good and not evil all the days of my life. I will extend my hand to those in need. I am clothed with strength and dignity. I will speak words of wisdom and kindness. I will fear the Lord and my deeds will speak for me.

Proverbs 31:10, 12, 20, 25, 26, 30, and 31

Day 15

CALL ME PRISCILLA

VIRGIE J. WASHINGTON

*Aquila and Priscilla greet you heartily in the
Lord, with the church that is in their house.*

1 CORINTHIANS 16:19

Have you ever heard of Priscilla? She was definitely a woman of strength and dignity, an unsung hero in the faith. Priscilla was a teacher, wife, and friend. Paul recognized her and her husband as helpers in Christ Jesus who put their necks on the line for him.

Priscilla taught alongside her husband when Apollos came from Ephesus. Although he was "an eloquent man and mighty in the Scriptures," Apollos was only acquainted with the baptism of John.

> When Aquila and Priscilla heard him, they took him aside and explained to him the way of God more accurately. (Acts 18:26)

Priscilla and her husband were always mentioned together. They were an inseparable team. By trade, they were tentmakers. Not only did they work side by side in business, but they served the Lord together. Priscilla and Aquila are mentioned only six times in the New Testament, but always with warm appreciation. It is apparent that they exemplified kindness and hospitality.

They were yoked together in life, love, and labor for Christ. They were what we would call a "power couple." What an example of partnership in ministry! They even started a church in their home. They gave God their hearts, their hands, and their home.

In so many ways, you can call me Priscilla. It brings so much joy to my life to walk beside my husband in both marriage and ministry. I am an ear when he simply needs someone to listen, and I am a hand when he needs help.

> Husband and wife are like the two equal parts of a soybean. If the two parts are put under the earth separately, they will not grow. The soybean will grow only when the parts are covered by the skin. Marriage is the skin which covers each of them and make them one. (Baba Hari Dass)

Maybe you are not married or in professional ministry, but every woman can be a Priscilla. The woman who invests her all in the kingdom. The woman who puts her neck on the line for the cause of Christ. The unsung hero who makes things happen.

You might be a Priscilla! The woman who goes the extra mile. The woman who does not need credit for the work of her hands. The woman to whom no job is too small, and nothing is beneath her. I love Priscilla!

> And whatever you do, do it heartily, as to the Lord and not to men. (Colossians 3:23)

THOUGHT FOR TODAY

I would like to be known as an intelligent woman, a courageous woman, a loving woman, a woman who teaches by being.

Maya Angelou

SCRIPTURE READING

Psalm 18:32

Proverbs 10:29

REFLECT

1. Discuss the value of women in the church.

2. How can we model Priscilla in our marriages and ministries?

3. What does it mean to be a team player in ministry?

TODAY'S PROMISE: LONGEVITY

Honor your father and your mother, so that you may live long in the land the LORD your God is giving you.

EXODUS 20:12 NIV

PRAYER

Lord, please give me the strength,
wisdom, and knowledge of Priscilla.
Help me to emulate her in my life. Amen.

ENCOURAGEMENT

Who will/did you encourage today? How?

GRATITUDE

Identify three things that you are thankful for.

1.

2.

3.

ME-GIFTING

How will/did you treat yourself today?
Remember the rule: You cannot spend any money!

MY DAILY PROVERBS 31 DECLARATION

I am a virtuous woman, and my worth is far above that of rubies. I will do good and not evil all the days of my life. I will extend my hand to those in need. I am clothed with strength and dignity. I will speak words of wisdom and kindness. I will fear the Lord and my deeds will speak for me.

PROVERBS 31:10, 12, 20, 25, 26, 30, AND 31

Day 16

TRUST YOUR GUT! LISTEN TO THE HOLY SPIRIT

JACQUELYN BAILEY WILLIAMS

"O Lord my God, you have performed many wonders for us. ... You take no delight in sacrifices or offerings. Now that you have made me listen, I finally understand."

PSALM 40:5A, 6A NLT

I have always wanted to be a woman who listens to God, whose "spiritual ears" are open. However, it becomes so easy to miss God speaking, because we can get so busy with our daily activities.

Sometimes it is hard for me to listen, to wait in the silence and hear nothing but the echoes of my thoughts, waiting for God to act and speak to me. But I had to learn the hard way that God is speaking all the time, even as the Spirit is moving and hovering over the troubled waters in my life. Yes, God is speaking! I had to realize I simply needed to listen to my gut instinct—or, as some may say, intuition—the thing that arises as a feeling within my body that only I experience. I want to be like the psalmist, to let God pierce my ear so that I might listen and learn to trust that small voice inside me: the Holy Spirit!

Speak to My Heart

A great lesson in listening is given to us in the story of Martha and

Mary. While Martha was concerned with housekeeping, fastidiously preparing a meal, and setting the right mood, Mary spent her time at Jesus' feet, listening to the Word. Having Jesus as a guest in their home must have been great. Nothing can surpass the life-giving, wound-healing, soul-comforting words of the Savior. Jesus punctuates the importance of listening as He tells Martha, "Mary has chosen that good part, which shall not be taken away from her" (Luke 10:42). We must be just like Mary, remembering that after the food has been consumed, the guests have gone home, and the dirty dishes have been washed, the Word remains.

Have you ever felt like God was speaking to you? Have you ever felt like you were missing the voice of God?

The story of Mary and Martha shows us two women whom Jesus loved dearly. But He would rather have both sitting at His feet while He fed their souls before they went out in the world to perform acts of service in His name. He wants us to be like Mary, listening to the Word!

Listen to the Holy Spirit

God desires to speak directly to us. As a good Father, He longs to engage with us in continual conversation. We can know His will, hear His voice, and live with the knowledge of His love. We need to take time to pull away from distractions and quiet our thoughts, even if it's just for ten to fifteen minutes. Let God speak to you, whether it's through a verse, a song, a person, or a whisper in your soul. Talk to Him about your plans for the day and ask Him to show you His, always giving Him permission to interrupt your thoughts and agenda and lead you in a different direction if He wants to. After you have done all this, get ready for a day filled with adventure and companionship as you walk hand-in-hand with your Maker.

THOUGHT FOR TODAY

God speaks in a soft voice; I can hear better when I resolve to listen and stop putting words in His mouth.

ELAINE ORABONA FOSTER

SCRIPTURE READING

Luke 11:28

John 8:47

Proverbs 1:5

REFLECT

1. Ask God what He wants you to focus on today.

2. List ways you can listen more closely to the Holy Spirit.

TODAY'S PROMISE: STRENGTH

He gives strength to the weary and increases the power of the weak.

Isaiah 40:29 niv

PRAYER

Thank You, Lord, for the blood of Jesus and the work of Your Holy Spirit. I proclaim that I will listen to the voice of the Lord and obey what He says. I proclaim His truth for me: "Obey My voice, and I will be your God." My body is a temple of the Holy Spirit, redeemed and cleansed by the blood of Jesus. Amen.

ENCOURAGEMENT

Who will/did you encourage today? How?

GRATITUDE

Identify three things that you are thankful for.

1.

2.

3.

ME-GIFTING

How will/did you treat yourself today?
Remember the rule: You cannot spend any money!

MY DAILY PROVERBS 31 DECLARATION

I am a virtuous woman, and my worth is far above that of rubies. I will do good and not evil all the days of my life. I will extend my hand to those in need. I am clothed with strength and dignity. I will speak words of wisdom and kindness. I will fear the Lord and my deeds will speak for me.

PROVERBS 31:10, 12, 20, 25, 26, 30, AND 31

Day 17

HELP ME RESUSCITATE MY PEACE

VICKIE BARBER-CARROLL

Finally, brothers and sisters, whatever is true, whatever is noble, whatever is right, whatever is pure, whatever is lovely, whatever is admirable—if anything is excellent or praiseworthy—think about such things. Whatever you have learned or received or heard from me, or seen in me—put it into practice. And the God of peace will be with you.

PHILIPPIANS 4:8–9 NIV

Storms don't just reflect the weather, they also happen in our everyday lives. James 1:2–3 tells us that trials and temptations will happen, and this trying of our faith will give us perseverance. Stress and storms are inevitable, but James in this text is in essence saying, "Count it all joy."

We all have triggers or things that disturb our peace; some things we deal with tactfully, while with others we're not so great. The trigger may be a co-worker, a friend, a fiancé, finances, or just life in general. The ways we will deal with these triggers can range from suffering severe depression to using those words that we teach our children not to use. Some of us even mask hard times with a smile.

Beginning to resuscitate my peace was undoubtedly all in my thinking. I had to stop thinking about my storms and focus on what tools God had already placed inside me to deal with those situations. Philippians 4:8 encourages us to get focused.

Adjust your thinking and make a list of what you can and cannot control. The biggest part for me was taking my personal feelings out of the scenario. Only focus your energy on what you are able to do or delegate.

We must also put our knowledge into action. A few years ago, I was forced to do just that! For each one of my storms, I had to focus on the blessing. My dad, who had always said he did not want to live dependent on machines, passed away. And my job was being phased out (I had been praying about a way out or a new opportunity). While a surgery kept me off work, I had plenty of paid leave and time to think. Paul admonishes us to put what God has taught us into practice. When we begin to think of His goodness, we have to stop stressing and start praising.

In all of this, Philippians 4:11 reminded me to be content in whatever state that I was in. I'd read that verse many times, but this time it struck me differently. Being content doesn't mean being complacent, but truly being present in the moment and recognizing God in it.

It was in my quiet moment that I realized that God had already given me what I needed to resuscitate my peace. Not everything is about us or how we feel. Resuscitating our peace is really about how we use the time and tools that God has given us. If we let God guide our thoughts and actions, we will find we have more time to enjoy life with less stress.

THOUGHT FOR TODAY

I'm no longer accepting the things I cannot change…
I'm changing the things I cannot accept.

ANGELA DAVIS

SCRIPTURE READING

Colossians 3:12

Luke 2:13-14

John 14:27

Romans 15:13

REFLECT

1. How can you practice the peace of God every day?

2. How can you set aside more time to discover the peace of God?

3. What distractions prevent you from keeping your mind on God and the perfect peace that He provides?

TODAY'S PROMISE: HELP

*For I am the L*ORD *your God who takes hold of your right hand and says to you, Do not fear; I will help you.*

ISAIAH 41:13 NIV

PRAYER

Lord, give me peace that surpasses all understanding. Let Your peace guard my mind and rule over my life. In the name of Jesus who is our peace, amen.

ENCOURAGEMENT

Who will/did you encourage today? How?

GRATITUDE

Identify three things that you are thankful for.

1.

2.

3.

ME-GIFTING

How will/did you treat yourself today?

Remember the rule: You cannot spend any money!

MY DAILY PROVERBS 31 DECLARATION

I am a virtuous woman, and my worth is far above that of rubies. I will do good and not evil all the days of my life. I will extend my hand to those in need. I am clothed with strength and dignity. I will speak words of wisdom and kindness. I will fear the Lord and my deeds will speak for me.

PROVERBS 31:10, 12, 20, 25, 26, 30, AND 31

Day 18

FORGETTING THE PAIN OF THE PAST

T. NICHOLE SPIES

*When Jesus had lifted up himself, and saw none but the
woman, he said unto her, Woman, where are those thine
accusers? hath no man condemned thee? She said, No
man, Lord. And Jesus said unto her, Neither do I condemn
thee: go, and sin no more. Then spake Jesus again unto them,
saying, I am the light of the world: he that followeth me
shall not walk in darkness, but shall have the light of life.*

JOHN 8:10–12 KJV

Every person has a past, some more painful than others. We have had experiences that have left us broken, wounded, and bound by the trauma we have endured. However, no matter what has happened, the only thing that can be done about it is to let go of the pain.

Yes, that is easier said than done, but you can do all things through Christ who gives you the strength to do so (Philippians 4:13). The Bible tells us that all have sinned and fallen short of the glory of God (Romans 3:23). The Word also tells us that we are new creations in Christ Jesus (2 Corinthians 5:17).

Our past should not keep us from living in the fullness of God today. When the woman was caught in adultery, the religious people wanted Jesus to pass judgment on her. According to the law of Moses, she deserved to be stoned.

Jesus, however, did not pass judgment. Scripture points out that He was writing in the sand and said, "He that is without sin among you let him first cast a stone at her" (John 8:7 KJV). When Jesus looked up, He asked the woman where her accusers were. Seeing that they were all gone, Jesus did not condemn the woman but told her to go and sin no more.

The only person that has power to judge is God. Jesus gave the woman a clean slate and simply told her to sin no more. It does not matter what people think about your past; what matters is that God says you are forgiven.

Pain has many meanings, one of which can be trouble or distress. You may not have caused the trouble or distress you have experienced; it may be the result of someone else's sins. No matter the origin of your pain, you have been given the opportunity through Christ to forget that pain. Jesus is waiting on you to lay it all at His feet so that you can be healed.

A part of getting past that pain is forgiveness—forgiveness of yourself and forgiveness for those who caused the pain. God wants to see you whole and living in the fullness of God. Today remind yourself of Psalm 147:3 (KJV): "He healeth the broken in heart, and bindeth up their wounds."

Be free today and allow God to heal your heart and bind your wounds. World-renowned author Tony Robbins once said, "Pain is a part of life. Suffering is an option." So, from this day forth declare and decree, "I will not allow the pain of my past to paralyze my present nor prevent me from progressing in my future."

THOUGHT FOR TODAY

Be passionate and move forward with gusto every single hour of every single day until you reach your goal.

AVA DUVERNAY

SCRIPTURE READING

Psalm 147:3

John 8:1–11

2 Corinthians 5:17

Philippians 4:13

Revelation 21:4

REFLECT

1. What pain in your past have you found hard to let go of?

2. What will you use from the lesson today to help you let go of that pain?

3. How will you use the pain of the past to help you walk in your purpose?

TODAY'S PROMISE: GOD'S PRESENCE

Keep your lives free from the love of money and be content with what you have, because God has said, "Never will I leave you; never will I forsake you." So we say with confidence, "The Lord is my helper; I will not be afraid. What can mere mortals do to me?"

HEBREWS 13:5–6 NIV

PRAYER

Lord, thank You for forgiving my past. I thank You that You have made me new, and I am free of the pain associated with my past. Lord, please give me the strength and dignity to continue walking in Your light as You guide me through this journey of life. Lord, help me to keep my eyes on You, never to look back with guilt and shame from the past. Lord, show me how to use the pain of my past to encourage other women and lead them to You. In Jesus' Name I thank You for the victory over the pain of my past. Amen.

ENCOURAGEMENT

Who will/did you encourage today? How?

GRATITUDE

Identify three things that you are thankful for.

1.

2.

3.

ME-GIFTING

How will/did you treat yourself today?
Remember the rule: You cannot spend any money!

MY DAILY PROVERBS 31 DECLARATION

I am a virtuous woman, and my worth is far above that of rubies. I will do good and not evil all the days of my life. I will extend my hand to those in need. I am clothed with strength and dignity. I will speak words of wisdom and kindness. I will fear the Lord and my deeds will speak for me.

PROVERBS 31:10, 12, 20, 25, 26, 30, AND 31

Day 11

THE ISSUE OF INSECURITY

NIKISHA DOTSON SMITH

I will praise thee; for I am fearfully and wonderfully made;
marvellous are thy works; and that my soul knoweth right well.

PSALM 139:14 KJV

Society has a narrow view of what is called "standard." Magazines, television, and social media display images of the perfect family, home, car, or body shape. This can lead us to compare ourselves to others and create insecurities.

What is insecurity? It is uncertainty or anxiety about oneself or the lack of confidence in oneself. Insecurity will cause you to seek validation, acceptance, and security from others.

When I was younger, I was full of confidence, energy, tenacity, and self-assurance, and I possessed a healthy curiosity. But along the way something happened. I started to listen and give too much attention to outside chatter. Gradually I became my own worst critic, full of insecurities. Why? Because I did not match the standard or the images around me. I did not fit in the box. The seed of insecurity entered my mind, and I had to battle with it.

To maximize our lives, we must see ourselves according to God's design and purpose for us. Proverbs 23:7 says, "For as he thinks in his heart, so is he." Henry Ford added, "Whether you think you can or you think you can't, you are right." Simply put, the battle is in the mind.

Encourage yourself daily. Take responsibility for nurturing confidence within. Discover all that is inside of you. You have purpose and power beyond your wildest imagination. Speak positive affirmations over yourself:

> I am made in the image of Christ.
>
> I am strong.
>
> I am whole.
>
> I love myself as I am.
>
> I appreciate all that I am and all that I have.
>
> I am capable.
>
> I am not a mistake.
>
> I am worthy, I am enough, and I am loved.
>
> My joy is not predicated on perfection but God's presence in my life.
>
> Fear, failure, and faithlessness are choices. Courage, love, and persistence are also choices.

Close your eyes. Envision yourself being, doing, and operating according to your greatest dreams—walking taller, receiving your degree, buying that home, going higher, and enjoying the fatness of the land.

Genesis 1:31 infers that all God's creation is good. Even with our flaws and limitations, we are good in God's sight. When you seek your standards from the Word, you win the battle against insecurity. It is then you can walk in self-acceptance, awareness, and love.

You have the potential to be a great mother, a phenomenal woman, a loving wife, an awesome woman in waiting, a caring daughter, and more. It all begins with you!

THOUGHTS FOR TODAY

Self-esteem means knowing you are the dream.

OPRAH WINFREY

*I need to see my own beauty and to continue to be reminded
that I am enough, that I am worthy of love without effort,
that I am beautiful, that the texture of my hair and that
the shape of my curves, the size of my lips, the color of my
skin, and the feelings that I have are all worthy and okay.*

TRACEE ELLIS ROSS

SCRIPTURE READING

Genesis 1:26–27

Psalm 139:14

Romans 8:37

Philippians 4:6–7

REFLECT

1. How are you fearfully and wonderfully made?

2. In what ways does the devil prey upon your insecurities?

3. How will you move past your insecurities to fulfill your divine purpose?

TODAY'S PROMISE: PROTECTION

*When you pass through the waters, I will be with you;
and when you pass through the rivers, they will not
sweep over you. When you walk through the fire, you will
not be burned; the flames will not set you ablaze.*

ISAIAH 43:2 NIV

PRAYER

Lord, You have anointed and created us for Your
glory. Help us to see and love ourselves according to
Your divine design. Everything about us has purpose
because You are an intentional God. God, in You we
lack nothing, and all things are made perfect. Break
the chains of insecurity, low self-esteem, and hatred.
Strengthen us to walk in the assurance that we are
fearfully and wonderfully made. In Jesus' name, amen.

ENCOURAGEMENT

Who will/did you encourage today? How?

GRATITUDE

Identify three things that you are thankful for.

1.

2.

3.

ME-GIFTING

How will/did you treat yourself today?

Remember the rule: You cannot spend any money!

MY DAILY PROVERBS 31 DECLARATION

I am a virtuous woman, and my worth is far above that of rubies. I will do good and not evil all the days of my life. I will extend my hand to those in need. I am clothed with strength and dignity. I will speak words of wisdom and kindness. I will fear the Lord and my deeds will speak for me.

PROVERBS 31:10, 12, 20, 25, 26, 30, AND 31

LOVE IN PLAIN SIGHT

CRYSTAL ROSE

When the Lord saw that Leah was not loved, he enabled her to conceive, but Rachel remained childless. Leah became pregnant and gave birth to a son. She named him Reuben, for she said, "It is because the Lord has seen my misery. Surely my husband will love me now." She conceived again, and when she gave birth to a son she said, "Because the Lord heard that I am not loved, he gave me this one too." So she named him Simeon. Again she conceived, and when she gave birth to a son she said, "Now at last my husband will become attached to me, because I have borne him three sons." So he was named Levi. She conceived again, and when she gave birth to a son she said, "This time I will praise the Lord." So she named him Judah. Then she stopped having children.

GENESIS 29:31–35 NIV

Life has ebbs and flows. At times we feel defeated by an unaccomplished goal or unfulfilled desires. The enemy can trick our minds into thinking we are failures.

Leah was the wife of Jacob. The marriage was out of obligation, not love. Jacob worked for Leah's father for seven years in hopes of marrying Leah's younger sister Rachel. During Leah and Jacob's marriage, she desperately wanted his love and affection, but he loved Rachel. Initially, Leah was barren, but then the Lord saw her need for love and blessed her with four sons. Leah thought that having children with Jacob would bring him closer to her, but unfortunately she didn't receive what she was expecting.

I once wanted to be loved by a person who didn't love me. During that time, I lacked self-esteem, confidence, and self-worth. In longing for love from a person, I fell victim to physical, mental, and verbal abuse.

While trying to cope with the fact that I was in an abusive relationship, like Leah I was looking to be loved when God loved me the entire time. So I prayed, and I noticed that my tears dried up and I regained my confidence. Similar to Leah, I stopped focusing on my immediate situation and realized God had bigger plans for my life.

Many women look for love in all the wrong places when God's love is all we need. We long for love from people who devalue us.

God blessed Leah before she even realized it. She was so captivated by the need to be loved by her husband that she missed God's work in action. God saw Leah's problem of being hated and loved less as an opportunity to show her what love was all about.

How often have you been in a situation where you felt that you were losing you? Your peace of mind? Self-worth and joy? Maybe you don't know who you are anymore, or you're so engulfed with the present that you've lost sight of the future. Be encouraged! Like Leah and me, it's not the end of your story.

Sometimes God uses our situations for our development. Leah misread God's blessing. The goal was to get closer to God, not Jacob. God is inviting us to enjoy Him and the peace that He offers.

Don't worry about anything, but in everything, through prayer and petition with thanksgiving, present your requests to God. And the peace of God, which surpasses all understanding, will guard your hearts and minds in Christ Jesus. (Philippians 4:6–7 CSB)

THOUGHT FOR TODAY

The best love story is one that is led by the author of love.

Author unknown

SCRIPTURE READING

Proverbs 31:30

Colossians 2:10

Luke 1:45

Psalm 73:26

REFLECT

1. What in your past has caused you to feel less than?

2. How can you embrace and embody the value that you have through Jesus Christ?

3. In what ways do you overlook the blessings of God?

TODAY'S PROMISE: COMPASSION

"Though the mountains be shaken and the hills be removed, yet my unfailing love for you will not be shaken nor my covenant of peace be removed," says the LORD, who has compassion on you.

ISAIAH 54:10 NIV

PRAYER

Lord, thank You for loving me beyond measure. Thank You for blessing me even though I may have overlooked it. Help me not to look for love from people, places, or things when Your love is in plain sight. In Jesus' name, amen!

ENCOURAGEMENT

Who will/did you encourage today? How?

GRATITUDE

Identify three things that you are thankful for.

1.

2.

3.

ME-GIFTING

How will/did you treat yourself today?

Remember the rule: You cannot spend any money!

MY DAILY PROVERBS 31 DECLARATION

I am a virtuous woman, and my worth is far above that of rubies. I will do good and not evil all the days of my life. I will extend my hand to those in need. I am clothed with strength and dignity. I will speak words of wisdom and kindness. I will fear the Lord and my deeds will speak for me.

PROVERBS 31:10, 12, 20, 25, 26, 30, AND 31

Day 21

AND I AM TELLING YOU I'M NOT GOING!

MONICA BLAKE MICKLE

But Ruth stayed with her.
RUTH 1:14 WEB

In the popular Broadway show *Dreamgirls*, the character Effie sings a song made popular by Jennifer Holiday. In part, she sings, "And I am telling you, I'm not going" as her declaration of love to the character Curtis Taylor, who dropped her from the fictional singing group The Dreamettes. Hundreds of years before this Broadway show was written, there was written in the Bible the account of a great woman named Ruth.

Ruth was married to one of the sons of Naomi. Unfortunately, Naomi's husband and both sons passed away and she was left with their wives in the land of Moab. Naomi decided she would return to her homeland and encouraged her sons' wives, Ruth and Orpha, to return to their families. Orpha obeyed but Ruth stayed with Naomi.

Ruth's willingness to stay with Naomi speaks volumes considering the proverbial mother-in-law/daughter-in-law relationship. Ruth was determined to make Naomi's family her family and Naomi's God her God.

Upon returning to Bethlehem, Naomi had a relative whose name was Boaz. Ruth knew she and Naomi had to be provided for, so she volunteered to go out and get grain from a local field that happened to belong to Boaz. Ruth found favor in that field. When Boaz found out she was a Moabite who had come back with Naomi, he encouraged Ruth to harvest only in his field. Boaz even encouraged his men to leave extra grain for her to harvest. Boaz would become the women's guardian-redeemer.

Boaz knew he was not the first male in the line of succession to be the guardian-redeemer, so he went to the man who was the head of that family to ask if he wanted to redeem Ruth and Naomi by purchasing the family's land and taking Ruth as his wife. Once it was established that the man was not interested, Boaz kept his word by purchasing the land and marrying Ruth. To their union was born a son to carry on the family's name.

That name is tied to the lineage of Jesus! When we honor God, God honors us. Because of Ruth's determination and dedication, she became a direct ancestor of Jesus.

Who or what do you cling to? Like Ruth, I suggest you stay close to the Redeemer who died so that each of us who receives Him would also become a descendant of Jesus.

THOUGHT FOR TODAY

Savior, let me walk close to thee.

FRANCES J. CROSBY

SCRIPTURE READING

Ruth 1

Psalm 91:4

1 Peter 5:7

REFLECT

1. Do the people you cling to exemplify godly lives that you are willing to follow?

2. Is God calling you to leave some people behind as you follow His will for your life?

TODAY'S PROMISE: FREEDOM

Is not this the kind of fasting I have chosen: to loose the chains of injustice and untie the cords of the yoke, to set the oppressed free and break every yoke?

ISAIAH 58:6 NIV

PRAYER

Dear God, today help me to recognize what to cling to and what should be cast aside. Help me to trust You and Your word to guide my thoughts and every direction I take. In Jesus' name, amen!

ENCOURAGEMENT

Who will/did you encourage today? How?

GRATITUDE

Identify three things that you are thankful for.

1.

2.

3.

ME-GIFTING

How will/did you treat yourself today?

Remember the rule: You cannot spend any money!

MY DAILY PROVERBS 31 DECLARATION

I am a virtuous woman, and my worth is far above that of rubies. I will do good and not evil all the days of my life. I will extend my hand to those in need. I am clothed with strength and dignity. I will speak words of wisdom and kindness. I will fear the Lord and my deeds will speak for me.

PROVERBS 31:10, 12, 20, 25, 26, 30, AND 31

Day 22

A WOMAN DESERVING OF PRAISE

MARYANNE MAIDEN

Charm is deceptive, and beauty is fleeting; but a woman who fears the Lord is to be praised.

PROVERBS 31:30 NIV

A woman rushed home from church ahead of everyone one evening to surprise the family by putting up Christmas lights on the outside of her home. As her family arrived, they were surprised but filled with laughter and jokes. Although her family never intended to be mean, the display of lights took them all by surprise. This light display wasn't what they were used to seeing. The woman's feelings were hurt, and she couldn't handle their disapproval of what she thought was a good deed. So, she went to her bedroom and cried. Unfortunately, this is what happens sometimes. Thank God that He sees our intentions and knows our hearts.

> The LORD doesn't see things the way you see them. People judge by outward appearance, but the LORD looks at the heart. (1 Samuel 16:7b NLT)

Beware of the exterior! Charm is deceptive. It is superficial. Even beauty is vain. However, there is nothing more virtuous than a woman who fears the Lord. Her reverence for God is seen in her worship, obedience, and service to others. Such women deserve praise.

We often look for praise from our husband or significant other, children, and sometimes our parents. The affirmation that we long for only comes from God. How amazing it is that God loves us even when we are at our worst.

A godly woman loves and fears the Lord. She has reverence for the Lord and is in awe of His holiness. She honors Him as God. She knows He deserves all the glory because He is the Lord of great glory, majesty, and power.

> Oh, fear the LORD, you his saints, for those who fear him have no lack! (Psalm 34:9 ESV)

The woman who fears God trusts Him with everything. Her inner beauty outshines her external beauty. She blesses others. She is humble and sensitive. If you know a woman like this, praise her and the Lord who made her.

Mothers, daughters, wives, sisters, and friends, fear the Lord and you shall be praised!

THOUGHT FOR TODAY

I realized that beauty was not a thing that I could acquire or consume, it was something I just had to be.

LUPITA NYONG'O

SCRIPTURE READING

1 Samuel 16:7

Luke 16:15

Jeremiah 17:10

REFLECT

1. How does it make you feel to know that God loves you even when you are at your worst?

2. How can you reverence God every day of your life?

3. In what ways can you teach other women that true beauty is not outward but inward?

TODAY'S PROMISE: WISDOM

If any of you lacks wisdom, you should ask God,
who gives generously to all without finding
fault, and it will be given to you.

JAMES 1:5 NIV

PRAYER

Heavenly Father, thank You for another opportunity to see
Your new mercies and a new day. I place all my trust in You,
Lord. You are the God of peace and love in whom I trust.
Please give me a peaceful heart and a kind spirit toward others.
Help me to be pleasing in Your sight. In Jesus' name, amen.

ENCOURAGEMENT

Who will/did you encourage today? How?

GRATITUDE

Identify three things that you are thankful for.

1.

2.

3.

ME-GIFTING

How will/did you treat yourself today?

Remember the rule: You cannot spend any money!

MY DAILY PROVERBS 31 DECLARATION

I am a virtuous woman, and my worth is far above that of rubies. I will do good and not evil all the days of my life. I will extend my hand to those in need. I am clothed with strength and dignity. I will speak words of wisdom and kindness. I will fear the Lord and my deeds will speak for me.

Proverbs 31:10, 12, 20, 25, 26, 30, and 31

Day 23

GOD'S FAVOR

BEVERLY H. HOUSTON

But seek first his kingdom and his righteousness, and
all these things will be given to you as well.

MATTHEW 6:33 NIV

During the spring of 1970, many graduating seniors, myself included, were making decisions about their next steps in life. Some would choose college or vocational schools. Others chose the military or employment with local businesses. Thank God for the people who provided good, sound advice. They played significant roles in our success.

My life has also been enriched by three noteworthy women in the Bible: Ruth, Esther, and Mary, the mother of Jesus. Ruth teaches us what it means to trust God in tough times. After the death of her husband, she chose to remain with Naomi. She made Naomi's God her God. Few stories exude God's favor more than Ruth's. In her, a widow became a winner!

Esther is a portrait of destiny. God placed her in the king's palace at a crucial time in the history of her Jewish people. Her story reads much like a fairy tale, but not quite. Typically, a prince comes along to rescue a damsel in distress. Esther saved an entire nation!

> She was powerful not because she wasn't scared but because she went on so strongly, despite the fear. (Atticus)

My heart gravitates to Mary, the mother of Jesus. In a very special way, I met her personally at the foot of the cross. It was there she agonized seeing the crucifixion of her son. I wept with her and she with me in the death of two of my sons. Mary is not only the mother of Jesus, she's a sister in sorrow. She introduced me to the strength that God gave her in a place no mother should ever have to visit. But because Mary's son lives, one day mine will too.

Like Ruth, I have experienced God's favor in despair. Like Esther, God's favor paved the way for my destiny. And like Mary, I found God's favor in a dark place. For me, the key to God's favor is seeking His kingdom first. It is then that everything that we need is added.

As a young college student who was a long way from home, I was never without God's protection, God's provisions, and God's peace. I was taught the conviction of Proverbs 3:5–6. It has been my security.

> Trust in the LORD with all your heart, And lean not on your own understanding; In all your ways acknowledge Him, And He shall direct your paths.

THOUGHT FOR TODAY

What God intended for you goes far beyond anything you can imagine.

OPRAH WINFREY

SCRIPTURE READING

Deuteronomy 6:4

Matthew 10:38–39

Colossians 3:17

REFLECT

1. What are some things that you find yourself putting before God?

2. How can you make God first in your life daily?

3. What has God added to your life since you put Him first?

TODAY'S PROMISE: JOY

You will show me the path of life; In Your presence is fullness of joy; At Your right hand are pleasures forevermore.

PSALM 16:11

PRAYER

God, our heavenly Father, we know that we are recipients of Your favor. It is unmerited but You are gracious. You extend Your lovingkindness to us in unbelievable ways. For that we are deeply grateful. In the name of Jesus, amen.

ENCOURAGEMENT

Who will/did you encourage today? How?

GRATITUDE

Identify three things that you are thankful for.

1.

2.

3.

ME-GIFTING

How will/did you treat yourself today?

Remember the rule: You cannot spend any money!

MY DAILY PROVERBS 31 DECLARATION

I am a virtuous woman, and my worth is far above that of rubies. I will do good and not evil all the days of my life. I will extend my hand to those in need. I am clothed with strength and dignity. I will speak words of wisdom and kindness. I will fear the Lord and my deeds will speak for me.

PROVERBS 31:10, 12, 20, 25, 26, 30, AND 31

Day 24

BE A BLESSING

SUNDRELL FARLEY ROSE

*Now there was in Joppa a disciple named Tabitha
... full of good works and acts of charity.*

ACTS 9:36 RSV

Perhaps you, like many, have struggled trying to find where you can best serve in the body of Christ. Perhaps you have tried to be a psalmist singing in the choir, or perhaps you have sought to be an usher showing worshippers into the church worship service.

There is an area where you can serve: the ministry of helps. When the apostle Paul wrote to the church in Corinth concerning gifts (1 Corinthians 12:28) he listed helping. Let's not seek the limelight and miss opportunities to "do good to others." As the old songs says, "May the work I've done speak for me."

The service given by women in the church is invaluable. Your service is invaluable. You can be a great blessing to many. Tabitha used her garment-making gift to make clothing for the poor. Like her, you can use your God-given gifts to help others.

What is the gift the Lord has given to you? What is it that you do well? What is it by which you wish to bless many? What is the God-given burden for others on your heart?

I am mindful of a woman in our church that is such a blessing. She encourages so many as she does all that she can to help, though she is sick with a very serious disease. She epitomizes the words of John Wesley:

I must do all of the good that I can, in all the ways that I can,
to as many people as I can, just as long as I can.

There are neither small people nor small gifts in the kingdom. It has been said that God uses stars and candles. Always be a blessing. Ask the Lord to order your steps guiding you to people for whom you can be a blessing. Submit to the will of God. Seek to glorify Him in all that you do.

I have never reached perfection, but I've tried. Sometimes
I have lost connections, but I have tried. Sometimes up,
sometimes down; sometimes I am leveled to the ground;
still I am climbing round by round, Lord knows I've tried.
(Williams E. Atkins)

THOUGHT FOR TODAY

*And whatever you do, in word or deed, do everything in the name
of the Lord Jesus, giving thanks to God the Father through him.*

COLOSSIANS 3:17 RSV

SCRIPTURE READING

Ephesians 2:10

Galatians 5:22–23

Romans 12:1–2

REFLECT

1. How can you use your spiritual gifts to bring glory to God?

2. In what way can you celebrate and appreciate the spiritual gifts of others?

TODAY'S PROMISE: FREEDOM FROM THE ENEMY

*Submit yourselves, then, to God. Resist the
devil, and he will flee from you.*

JAMES 4:7 NIV

PRAYER

Lord, help me to know and to do Your will for my
life to the end that Christ is glorified. Amen.

ENCOURAGEMENT

Who will/did you encourage today? How?

GRATITUDE

Identify three things that you are thankful for.

1.

2.

3.

ME-GIFTING

How will/did you treat yourself today?
Remember the rule: You cannot spend any money!

MY DAILY PROVERBS 31 DECLARATION

I am a virtuous woman, and my worth is far above that of rubies. I will do good and not evil all the days of my life. I will extend my hand to those in need. I am clothed with strength and dignity. I will speak words of wisdom and kindness. I will fear the Lord and my deeds will speak for me.

PROVERBS 31:10, 12, 20, 25, 26, 30, AND 31

Day 25

GOD'S MASTERPIECE

ANGELA LACEY

*For we are God's masterpiece. He has created us anew in Christ
Jesus, so we can do the good things he planned for us long ago.*

EPHESIANS 2:10 NLT

Y ou are God's masterpiece. What does it mean to be a masterpiece?
The Merriam-Webster Dictionary defines the word masterpiece as
"a work done with extraordinary skill." Other sources define masterpiece as "a work of outstanding artistry, workmanship, or mastery skill."
These definitions reveal powerful characteristics of an artist's work as a
metaphor for who we are as children of God.

A masterpiece reflects the artist's thoughts and emotions. Like a
dancer performing on stage or a musician delivering a musical piece,
their artistry is an expression of their own thoughts inspired by something deep within. It is a direct expression of what they may think
and/or feel. Just like God expresses to Jeremiah, "I knew you before I
formed you in your mother's womb" (Jeremiah 1:5 NLT), God knew
His plan for you before He formed you!

Of all the characteristics of a masterpiece that we find in the many
definitions provided, I noticed that perfection is not one of them.
Understand that we will never enter full perfection until we reach
heaven. None of us are flawless and we are all works in progress.

The true beauty of a masterpiece is often not in its perfection, but
in its uniqueness. An artist's masterpiece rarely has duplicates, and

what makes us uniquely different is what makes us beautiful. Even if an artist performs the same choreography more than once or paints a bowl of fruit more than once, it rarely comes out exactly the same. God—the Master—did not create you to be ordinary, but extraordinary! David declares, "Thank you for making me so wonderfully complex! Your workmanship is marvelous—how well I know it" (Psalm 139:14 NLT).

God even uses your trials as a part of His artistry to make you new, so that you can do the awesome things He has planned for you since the beginning of time. Paul reminds us in Romans 8:29 (NLT), "For God knew his people in advance, and he chose them to become like his Son."

God has had awesome things for us to do since the beginning of time! Each day He is bringing us one step closer to accomplishing those things. An excellent self-esteem booster is knowing who you are in Christ. As God's masterpiece you are enough. You are worthy of His love, grace, and mercy! You are beautiful!

THOUGHT FOR TODAY

A star does not compete with other stars around it. It just shines.

MATSHONA DHLIWAYO

SCRIPTURE READING

Psalm 139:14

Isaiah 64:8

Jeremiah 1:5

REFLECT

1. How do you honestly feel about yourself?

2. How does God feel about you?

3. What good things does God have planned for you?

TODAY'S PROMISE: FORGIVENESS

*If we confess our sins, he is faithful and just and will forgive
us our sins and purify us from all unrighteousness.*

1 JOHN 1:9 NIV

PRAYER

Dear God, thank You for making me so wonderfully unique.
Help me continue to discover the plans You have for me.
Strengthen me in the areas that need refining so that I can
display Your outstanding artistry. Thank You for loving me
enough to illuminate Your love, grace, and mercy. Amen.

ENCOURAGEMENT

Who will/did you encourage today? How?

GRATITUDE

Identify three things that you are thankful for.

1.

2.

3.

ME-GIFTING

How will/did you treat yourself today?

Remember the rule: You cannot spend any money!

MY DAILY PROVERBS 31 DECLARATION

I am a virtuous woman, and my worth is far above that of rubies. I will do good and not evil all the days of my life. I will extend my hand to those in need. I am clothed with strength and dignity. I will speak words of wisdom and kindness. I will fear the Lord and my deeds will speak for me.

PROVERBS 31:10, 12, 20, 25, 26, 30, AND 31

Day 26

GO FOR THE G.O.L.D.

RENEE M. WHITE

*Brethren, I count not myself to have apprehended: but this one
thing I do, forgetting those things which are behind, and reaching
forth unto those things which are before. I press toward the
mark for the prize of the high calling of God in Christ Jesus.*

PHILIPPIANS 3:13–14 KJV

E very four years the world comes together to watch the global multi-sport event known as the Olympic Games. These games open with the host nation welcoming the world's greatest athletes at the top of their sports. These athletes have trained tirelessly with blood, sweat, and tears, having earned their spot at a chance to be named best in the world. They are there to "go for the gold."

As you run this Christian race, I encourage you to stay focused on your journey. I encourage you to stay on the narrow path and remember to "go for the gold."

G = God, O = Obey, L = Love, D = Disciple

G = God, seek Him

In this world there are so many things that distract us, such as family, friends, and Facebook. Because we lead busy lives, we can easily go days without "checking in" with our Father. We must be keenly aware of the traps Satan sets that keep us from that narrow path.

Seek the Lord and His strength, seek His face continually. (1 Chronicles 16:11 KJV)

O = Obey Him

Growing up, I used to hear my parents say to me and my siblings, "Obedience is better than sacrifice." Just like a loving parent, God our Father gives us His instructions for our lives. All we need do is read and obey His word.

If you love Me, keep My commandments. (John 14:15)

L = Love others

The greatest commandment is that we love one another. Love is putting the wants and needs of others above your own. Real love, the kind God requires of believers, is sacrificial. We have the greatest example in Jesus, who became a living sacrifice for us.

Greater love hath no man than this, that a man lay down his life for his friends. (John 15:13 KJV)

D = Disciple others

This is a commandment given to us in Matthew 28, when Jesus gave instructions to his disciples before He ascended to His Father. He told them to make disciples as they went out into the world, and to baptize them and teach them. As ambassadors for the kingdom, our duty is to disciple others and bring them into the fold.

You are the light of the world. (Matthew 5:14)

"Go for the GOLD"

As believers, we "go for the gold" when we seek God, obey His commandments, love one another, and disciple others. When all is said and done, wouldn't you like to hear the Master say, "Well done, thy good and faithful servant"?

THOUGHTS FOR TODAY

You don't make progress by standing on the sidelines, whimpering, and complaining. You make progress by implementing ideas.

SHIRLEY CHISHOLM

One of the lessons that I grew up with was to always stay true to yourself and never let what somebody else says distract you from your goals.

MICHELLE OBAMA

SCRIPTURE READING

Hebrews 12:1–2

1 Corinthians 9:24–27

Isaiah 40:31

REFLECT

1. What in your past is keeping you from your divine destiny?

2. How can you press toward the mark of the high calling of Jesus daily?

TODAY'S PROMISE: SALVATION

For God so loved the world that he gave his one and only Son, that whoever believes in him shall not perish but have eternal life.

JOHN 3:16 NIV

PRAYER

Lord, no matter how hard it may be,
help me to press and fight. Amen.

ENCOURAGEMENT

Who will/did you encourage today? How?

GRATITUDE

Identify three things that you are thankful for.

1.

2.

3.

ME-GIFTING

How will/did you treat yourself today?
Remember the rule: You cannot spend any money!

MY DAILY PROVERBS 31 DECLARATION

I am a virtuous woman, and my worth is far above that
of rubies. I will do good and not evil all the days of my
life. I will extend my hand to those in need. I am clothed
with strength and dignity. I will speak words of wisdom and
kindness. I will fear the Lord and my deeds will speak for me.

Proverbs 31:10, 12, 20, 25, 26, 30, and 31

Day 27

WHAT HUMILITY
LOOKS LIKE

THERESA SMITH

*When Abigail saw David, she quickly got off
her donkey and bowed low before him.*

1 SAMUEL 25:23 NLT

Today's women occupy more leadership roles than ever before. These roles may be in our professions, communities, churches, or households, and most often are in a combination of all the above.

In juggling responsibilities, stress is always near. We want to be our best at everything and for everyone. In this quest for perfection, we often hide behind the persona of being strong. That can leave little room for humility.

> Be completely humble and gentle; be patient, bearing with
> one another in love. (Ephesians 4:2 NIV)

Those in my generation remember the television show *The Odd Couple*. The terribly opposite personalities of Oscar and Felix produced tons of conflict and laughter. Abigail and her husband Nabal were the Old Testament's odd couple. There was definitely conflict, but no laughter!

Abigail and Nabal could not have been more different. Abigail was beautiful, wise, and godly. Maya Angelou would call her "a phenomenal woman." She was definitely "clothed with strength and dignity."

Nabal, on the other hand, was something else! Nabal's name means "fool"—and that he was! Nabal was wealthy but mean and impolite. He might have even been an alcoholic.

After Nabal denied David's army food and supplies, David vowed to kill him and his entire household. When Abigail heard of David's plan, she went to David and humbly apologized for her husband's arrogant breach of hospitality.

Abigail prevented David from destroying Nabal, but she could not prevent Nabal from destroying himself. When she returned, Nabal was in a drunken stupor. The next day, she told him what she had done. The Bible says, "His heart died within him." He laid flat on his back "like a stone" for ten days before he expired (1 Samuel 25:37–38).

> Pride goes before destruction, a haughty spirit before a fall.
> (Proverbs 16:18 NIV)

In pride, Nabal did what he thought was right.
In humility, Abigail did what was actually right.

THOUGHT FOR TODAY

I want to be a woman that offers what I know with grace and accepts what I don't know with humility.

WENDY POPE

SCRIPTURE READING

Ephesians 4:32

Psalm 116:5

Proverbs 11:16

REFLECT

1. How can you prevent pride from getting the best of you?

2. How can you be like Abigail and extend grace to others?

TODAY'S PROMISE: GLOBAL HEALING

If my people, who are called by my name, will humble themselves and pray and seek my face and turn from their wicked ways, then I will hear from heaven, and I will forgive their sin and will heal their land.

2 Chronicles 7:14 niv

PRAYER

Lord, help me to have the spirit of Abigail when I have an opportunity to bless others. Amen.

ENCOURAGEMENT

Who will/did you encourage today? How?

GRATITUDE

Identify three things that you are thankful for.

1.

2.

3.

ME-GIFTING

How will/did you treat yourself today?

Remember the rule: You cannot spend any money!

MY DAILY PROVERBS 31 DECLARATION

I am a virtuous woman, and my worth is far above that of rubies. I will do good and not evil all the days of my life. I will extend my hand to those in need. I am clothed with strength and dignity. I will speak words of wisdom and kindness. I will fear the Lord and my deeds will speak for me.

PROVERBS 31:10, 12, 20, 25, 26, 30, AND 31

Day 28

TAKE A LICKING AND KEEP ON TICKING

LOIS THOMAS

We are hard pressed on every side, but not crushed;
perplexed, but not in despair; persecuted, but not
abandoned; struck down, but not destroyed.

2 CORINTHIANS 4:8–9 NIV

Several decades ago, there was a commercial about a sturdy and dependable watch. The announcer, John Swayze, did several commercials demonstrating the stability and sturdiness of the Timex watch. He popularized the slogan: "It takes a licking and keeps on ticking."

Job 14:1 (KJV) promises, "Man that is born of a woman is of few days and full of trouble." You might agree—IT IS ALWAYS SOMETHING! No one escapes trials and tribulations. I personally know this all too well. A few years ago, we lost a child suddenly to a heart attack. One month later, a second child had a triple-bypass heart surgery. The next year, our daughter was diagnosed with cancer. I lost my mother the year after that. My life began to resemble that of Job.

Thank God for His Word! It embraced me when I did not have the strength to embrace it. Philippians 4 took on a new meaning for me. I have literally learned to be content in whatever state I am. I know what it is to take a licking and keep on ticking.

It was rough, but I leaned on Philippians 4:13. Today I know that "I can do all things through Christ which strengthens me." I know that I can trust in the Lord with all my heart. Today I can acknowledge Him in the good, the bad, and the ugly. Even in my hurt, God directed my path.

I often reflect on a song by the late Reverend Paul Jones:

> I've had some good days.
> I've some hills to climb.
> I've had some weary days,
> And some sleepless nights.
> But when I, when I look around
> And I think things over.
> All of my good days
> Outweigh my bad days.
> I won't complain!
> *Why?*
> Because He knows what's best for me.

Much of life is a about one's mindset. Whatever our plight, let's recognize God as the source of our strength. Always remember that we are "clothed with strength and dignity." See your struggle as the introduction to strength unknown.

> And the God of all grace, who called you to his eternal glory in Christ, after you have suffered a little while, will himself restore you and make you strong, firm and steadfast. (1 Peter 5:10 NIV)

> Every difficulty you face, in every waiting place, you're being given the chance to trust in the things unseen and to be abundantly blessed. (Cherie Hill)

> If you have to take a licking, just keep on ticking!

--- **THOUGHT FOR TODAY** ---

Where there is no struggle, there is no strength.

OPRAH WINFREY

SCRIPTURE READING

John 14:1

Romans 8:28

Isaiah 43:2

REFLECT

1. What have you learned from life's hurt and pain?

2. What can you do to keep your condition from controlling your state of mind?

TODAY'S PROMISE: ETERNAL LIFE

Whoever believes in the Son has eternal life, but whoever rejects the Son will not see life, for God's wrath remains on them.

JOHN 3:36 NIV

PRAYER

Father, give me strength to get back up
when life knocks me down! Amen.

ENCOURAGEMENT

Who will/did you encourage today? How?

GRATITUDE

Identify three things that you are thankful for.

1.

2.

3.

ME-GIFTING

How will/did you treat yourself today?

Remember the rule: You cannot spend any money!

MY DAILY PROVERBS 31 DECLARATION

I am a virtuous woman, and my worth is far above that of rubies. I will do good and not evil all the days of my life. I will extend my hand to those in need. I am clothed with strength and dignity. I will speak words of wisdom and kindness. I will fear the Lord and my deeds will speak for me.

PROVERBS 31:10, 12, 20, 25, 26, 30, AND 31

BROKEN BUT NOT DEFEATED

YULANDA BLACKSHIRE

*"Don't call me Naomi," she told them. "Call me Mara,
because the almighty has made my life very bitter."*
RUTH 1:20 NIV

Naomi is the woman who has lost everything. She is broken, grieving the loss of her husband and both sons. She is bitter. She even insists on being called Mara, which means "bitter." Naomi is also empty. Are you Naomi?

Naomis are everywhere! They have survived abuse, neglect, and grief. They have endured failed relationships, financial distress, and traumatic experiences. They have conquered depression and disappointments. Once upon a time, I was Naomi!

Many of us have experienced challenging situations that have left us broken, hurt, disappointed, and perhaps even depressed. We can only imagine the depths of Naomi's emotions. Naomi was at the crossroad of her life, feeling despondent and empty. She was in a dark place.

"I went away full, and the Lord has brought me back empty."
(Ruth 1:21 NIV)

Being in a dark place can be frightening and sometimes devastating. Dark, bitter places blind us to the hand of God, Who is at work in all things for our good (Romans 8:28).

> A woman's strength is not just about how much she can handle before she breaks, it's also about how much she must handle after she is broken. (J. S. Scott)

In that dark, bitter place, Naomi may not have felt the presence of God. However, Naomi was never alone. Deuteronomy 31:8 (NIV) promises, "The Lord himself goes before you and will be with you; he will never leave you nor forsake you. Do not be afraid; do not be discouraged."

God strategically placed Ruth in Noami's life to help her through her dim moments. Ruth assured Naomi, "Where you go I will go, and where you stay I will stay. Your people will be my people and your God my God" (Ruth 1:16 NIV).

At the beginning of the story, Naomi lost everything. At the end of the story, Naomi embraces the newborn son of Ruth and Boaz. His name was Obed, the father of Jesse, the father of David, the king of Israel. Ruth's victory was Naomi's victory.

I was Naomi.

I was bitter.

Today, I am better, and you can be too!

THOUGHT FOR TODAY

It's not the load that breaks you down, it's the way you carry it.

LENA HORNE

SCRIPTURE READING

Psalm 40:2–3

Psalm 42:5

Ephesians 4:31

REFLECT

1. Describe a time when you did not feel the presence of God.

2. How did God show up in that situation?

3. What can we learn from the story of Naomi?

TODAY'S PROMISE: DELIVERANCE

So if the Son sets you free, you will be free indeed.
JOHN 8:36 NIV

PRAYER

Lord, sometimes life is overwhelming and too much for us to bear. I am thankful that even during the times we may not be able to trace You, we know we can always trust You. Amen.

ENCOURAGEMENT

Who will/did you encourage today? How?

GRATITUDE

Identify three things that you are thankful for.

1.

2.

3.

ME-GIFTING

How will/did you treat yourself today?

Remember the rule: You cannot spend any money!

MY DAILY PROVERBS 31 DECLARATION

I am a virtuous woman, and my worth is far above that of rubies. I will do good and not evil all the days of my life. I will extend my hand to those in need. I am clothed with strength and dignity. I will speak words of wisdom and kindness. I will fear the Lord and my deeds will speak for me.

PROVERBS 31:10, 12, 20, 25, 26, 30, AND 31

Day 30

I SEE IT ALL NOW

SHERBRINA T. JONES

*Yes, I see it all now: I'm the Lord's maid, ready
to serve. Let it be with me just as you say.*

LUKE 1:38 MSG

During my childhood, I only wanted to blend in. I was totally comfortable with what society labeled as normal. I thought "average" was a safe place. Why? It is easy for average people to get lost in the crowd. I was OK being there because I did not think that anyone would notice me.

Maybe that is how Mary felt. She was just an average Jewish girl engaged to a carpenter. Mary and her husband Joseph may not have ever envisioned anything other than a normal life in their humble town of Nazareth. Little did they know that God had other plans!

Mary got an unexpected visit from an angel that gave her a new vision of herself. He said, "Rejoice, highly favored one, the Lord is with you; blessed *are* you among women!" (Luke 1:28). In the eyes of God, Mary was so much more than a teenaged peasant from a lowly community.

As Mary was bewildered, the angel relieved Mary's fears, saying "Do not be afraid, Mary; you have found favor with God" (Luke 1:30 NIV). The angel also confirmed Mary's purpose:

> You will conceive and give birth to a son, and you are to call
> him Jesus. He will be great and will be called the Son of the

Most High. The Lord God will give him the throne of his father David, and he will reign over Jacob's descendants forever; his kingdom will never end. (Luke 1:31–33 NIV)

To be "blessed and highly favored" is not just a cliché or expression. It is a calling—and everyone has one! It is to wholeheartedly surrender to God's will for your life. Mary was called to deliver the man who will deliver us all.

> We can find joy in knowing that God's favor is greater than our fear.

Maya Angelou said, "Hope and fear cannot occupy the same space, invite one to stay." I chose to kick fear out of the door. Like Mary, I was never average. Those thoughts were a waste of time.

Like Mary, I was called to be a servant of God. I was destined to encourage others to be great. Every day I extend the healing hands of Jesus through nursing and today I am encouraging you to be a willing servant like Mary.

> The woman who serves unnoticed and un-thanked is a woman who loves God more than she desires the praise of others. (Wendy Pope)

Say yes to God's will for your life. Believe that you can conquer anything. There is a blessing in obedience, and in the end God will be glorified.

THOUGHT FOR TODAY

I have learned over the years that when one's mind is made up, this diminishes fear; knowing what must be done does away with fear.

ROSA PARKS

SCRIPTURE READING

Proverbs 3:5–6

Jeremiah 29:11

2 Timothy 1:7

1 Peter 4:10

REFLECT

1. In what ways have you allowed fear to dominate your life?

2. What prevents you from totally surrendering to God's will for your life?

3. Do you know what your spiritual gifts are?

4. How can you use your gifts to bless others?

TODAY'S PROMISE: FINANCIAL BLESSING

"Bring the whole tithe into the storehouse, that there may be food in my house. Test me in this," says the LORD Almighty, "and see if I will not throw open the floodgates of heaven and pour out so much blessing that there will not be room enough to store it."

MALACHI 3:10 NIV

PRAYER

Dear Lord, help us to not have the spirit of fear. Give us power, a heart of love, and a sound mind so that we can be prosperous servants for You. Amen!

ENCOURAGEMENT

Who will/did you encourage today? How?

GRATITUDE

Identify three things that you are thankful for.

1.

2.

3.

ME-GIFTING

How will/did you treat yourself today?
Remember the rule: You cannot spend any money!

MY DAILY PROVERBS 31 DECLARATION

I am a virtuous woman, and my worth is far above that of rubies. I will do good and not evil all the days of my life. I will extend my hand to those in need. I am clothed with strength and dignity. I will speak words of wisdom and kindness. I will fear the Lord and my deeds will speak for me.

PROVERBS 31:10, 12, 20, 25, 26, 30, AND 31

Day 31

TRUSTING GOD
IN TOUGH TIMES

TOMIKO FULLER CAIN

*Trust in the LORD with all thine heart; and lean
not unto thine own understanding. In all thy ways
acknowledge him, and he shall direct thy paths.*

PROVERBS 3:5–6 KJV

Tough times never last but tough people do.

ROBERT H. SCHULLER

Faith is believing or trusting in the knowledge or ability of someone else. Though we are people of faith, our lives are filled with difficulties, problems, and uncertainties. Every one of us has either just passed through a crisis, is facing a crisis, or is headed into one.

Whether you face financial distress, bereavement, or a family issue—it is ALWAYS something! Crises often produce changes, and those changes can lead to growth. Children of God can rest assured that God is at work even in these tough times.

> And we know that all things work together for good to
> those who love God, to those who are the called according
> to His purpose. (Romans 8:28)

It is not always easy to face difficulties or challenges in life. However, the one thing that we can always do is trust God. We can place our faith in God and stand firm in Him. There are even times when we must encourage ourselves as David did.

As believers, we can find comfort in knowing that no crisis will last forever. Think about all the things that we have survived in the past. They are done, but we are not! We are still here because we are "more than conquerors" (Romans 8:37). While we cannot handle everything, our God can!

> Fear not, for I am with you; Be not dismayed, for I am your God. I will strengthen you, Yes, I will help you, I will uphold you with My righteous right hand. (Isaiah 41:10)

> What a friend we have in Jesus,
> All our sins and griefs to bear!
> What a privilege to carry
> Everything to God in prayer!

> Oh, what peace we often forfeit,
> Oh, what needless pain we bear,
> All because we do not carry
> Everything to God in prayer!

> (Joseph M. Scriven)

There is not a more convincing story of faith in action than the woman who had an issue of blood for twelve years. Even after spending all that she had on physicians the Bible says she only got worse. We meet her in Matthew 9 with one thing left: her faith. And that would be all that she needed!

She believed that if she could only touch the hem of Jesus' garment that she would be made whole. She pressed through the crowd, did just that, and "was made well from that hour" (Matthew 9:22). Like this woman and so many others, you can trust God in tough times.

Our foreparents always sang, "He may not come when you want Him but He's always on time." In the movie *The Case for Christ*, Alfie said, "In His time and in His way, God always keeps His promises."

THOUGHT FOR TODAY

Don't worry. God is never blind to your tears, deaf to your prayers, or silent to your pain. He sees, He hears, and He will deliver you.

AUTHOR UNKNOWN

SCRIPTURE READING

Isaiah 40:31

2 Corinthians 1:3

Philippians 4:13

REFLECT

1. How can we shift our focus from our problems to the goodness of God?

2. When did God show up and bring you through a difficult time in your life?

TODAY'S PROMISE: SOUND MIND

For God has not given us a spirit of fear, but of power and of love and of a sound mind.

2 TIMOTHY 1:7

PRAYER

Lord, help me to trust You even in bad times. Amen.

ENCOURAGEMENT

Who will/did you encourage today? How?

GRATITUDE

Identify three things that you are thankful for.

1.

2.

3.

ME-GIFTING

How will/did you treat yourself today?

Remember the rule: You cannot spend any money!

MY DAILY PROVERBS 31 DECLARATION

I am a virtuous woman, and my worth is far above that of rubies. I will do good and not evil all the days of my life. I will extend my hand to those in need. I am clothed with strength and dignity. I will speak words of wisdom and kindness. I will fear the Lord and my deeds will speak for me.

PROVERBS 31:10, 12, 20, 25, 26, 30, AND 31

THE COURAGE OF DEBORAH

T. NICHOLE SPIES

Then Barak said to her, "If you will go with me, then I will go; but if you will not go with me, I will not go." She said, "I will certainly go with you; nevertheless, the journey that you are about to take will not be for your honor and glory, because the Lord will sell Sisera into the hand of a woman." Then Deborah got up and went with Barak to Kedesh.

JUDGES 4:89 AMP

Deborah was strong and courageous in a time when it was not very popular for women to be in the forefront. She was a judge over the people of Israel and a prophetess of the Lord. She sat daily at the palm tree of Deborah as she, in her wisdom, judged the people of Israel with the guidance of the Spirit of God. Deborah's courage and wisdom earned the respect of all, including the general of Israel's army, Barak, who refused to go into battle unless she stood by his side. God used her to help his people break free from twenty years of bondage under the rule of King Jabin of Canaan after the Israelites had sinned.

Not once throughout this story does Deborah allow fear or the concerns of others to cause her to waver from what God had spoken to her. She was attentive to the voice of God and moved as He instructed her to instruct His people. We can be afraid to move when God speaks, if what He's asking us to do is out of the norm. Fear has stopped so many women from pursing and achieving the vision that God has given them. 2 Timothy 1:7 says, "For God has not given us a spirit of fear, but of power and of love and of a sound mind."

Be encouraged today and tap into that power. Oprah Winfrey once said, "What God intends for you goes far beyond anything you can imagine." Rise above those fears and dream-killers that try to take away your courage. Tell the armies of doubt and the commanders of fear that you come in the Name of the Lord, and you will no longer be held in bondage to your fear because you are a woman of strength and dignity. Remind your fears of Deuteronomy 31:6 and tell yourself, "I will be strong and of good courage. I will not fear, nor be afraid of my enemies. God is with me; he will not fail nor forsake me." Let today be the beginning of you listening to God and allowing the Holy Spirit to guide you in fulfilling those dreams and desires that God has placed in you.

THOUGHT FOR TODAY

No matter the task or trial, I will have courage to prevail, because God is always with me, and He is my source and strength.

SCRIPTURE READING

Judges 4–5

Deuteronomy 31:6

Joshua 1:9

1 Chronicles 28:20

1 Corinthians 16:13

2 Timothy 1:7

REFLECT

1. What has kept you captive from walking in courage?

2. What does courage through Christ mean to you?

3. How can you walk in courage today?

TODAY'S PROMISE: ENCOURAGEMENT

Have I not commanded you? Be strong and courageous.
Do not be afraid; do not be discouraged, for the LORD
your God will be with you wherever you go.

JOSHUA 1:9 NIV

PRAYER

Lord, I thank You that You have not given me a spirit of fear but of love, power, and a sound mind. Father, strengthen me and guide me to be a woman of courage, facing my fears head on. I thank You for giving me courage, dignity, and strength so that I may pursue my dreams and yield to Your purpose for my life. In Jesus' name I claim victory over my fears. Amen.

ENCOURAGEMENT

Who will/did you encourage today? How?

GRATITUDE

Identify three things that you are thankful for.

1.

2.

3.

ME-GIFTING

How will/did you treat yourself today?

Remember the rule: You cannot spend any money!

MY DAILY PROVERBS 31 DECLARATION

I am a virtuous woman, and my worth is far above that of rubies. I will do good and not evil all the days of my life. I will extend my hand to those in need. I am clothed with strength and dignity. I will speak words of wisdom and kindness. I will fear the Lord and my deeds will speak for me.

PROVERBS 31:10, 12, 20, 25, 26, 30, AND 31

WHAT ARE YOU DOING HERE?

NICOLE EASON

What are you doing here, Elijah?
1 Kings 19:13 niv

Have you ever been driving and suddenly think, "How did I get here?" That can happen in our lives. We can become so focused on balancing spiritual life, marriage, career, and family that we neglect to see that we are moving away from God—until suddenly you hear God say, "What are you doing here?"

At Mount Carmel, God showed His power by consuming the altar and killing all the prophets of Baal. Instead of standing in his assigned place, Elijah ran and hid in a cave in fear. He was afraid of what he thought Jezebel would do to him. God did not grant Elijah's request for death but sent an angel to feed him.

While in the cave, a strong wind blew, an earthquake came, and a fire broke out. It was not until after the fire that Elijah heard God speak. God will use situations to get our attention and our focus back on Him. Sometimes that's the only time some of us actually "hear" God.

I remember a time when I found myself in an unassigned place. My husband and I (mostly me) thought it would be a good idea for me to get a job. I was pregnant and had two toddlers. We could definitely use the extra income!

My husband and I worked in the same place. We would take turns dropping the kids off at daycare, and things were functioning well, until one day. I got up like normal, packed the kids' bags, put everybody in the car, and took off on I-635 to Irving, Texas.

I pulled into the parking lot at work and jumped out of the car. Before the door closed, I heard my son's small voice say, "This is where Mommy and Daddy work." I was so focused on the traffic and getting to work that I neglected to drop the kids off at daycare.

It was not until I parked and got out of the car that I heard my son speak. Understand this is Dallas, Texas, in the middle of the summer, with 100-degree-plus temperatures, and I was about to lock my kids in the car and go to work for an eight-hour shift. How did I get here?

On my way home, I heard the small voice again, this time saying, "Mommy don't cry, it's all better." I didn't realize at the time that God used my son's voice to tell me that I was not in my assigned place. The assignment that God had given me was to be a wife and mother, not a specimen-processing clerk at a lab. This is what I wanted. This is what my husband and I thought we needed for the family. It was God's voice telling me that even in the decision to go back to work, He was still right there with me, and everything would be all right.

I continued to work, but with my focus on God and not on my wants. Like God telling Elijah to go back, eventually I had to go back to my assigned place, and I thank God for every moment.

God has assigned a task for each one of us. My assignment may not be the same as your assignment. It is so easy to get distracted by our own desires that we lose focus. Let's keep the main thing the main thing.

> And let us not grow weary in well-doing, for in due season
> we shall reap, if we do not lose heart. (Galatians 6:9 RSV)

THOUGHT FOR TODAY

Faith is the first factor in a life devoted to service. Without it, nothing is possible. With it, nothing is impossible.

MARY MCLEOD BETHUNE

SCRIPTURE READING

1 Kings 19

Jeremiah 29:11

Psalm 34:17–18

REFLECT

1. Have you ever asked yourself, "What in the world am I doing here?"

2. Are you in the assigned place that God has given you? What is that place? And how did you get there?

3. Thank God for knowing you and the plans that He has for you.

TODAY'S PROMISE: SUFFICIENCY

And my God will meet all your needs according to the riches of his glory in Christ Jesus.

PHILIPPIANS 4:19 NIV

PRAYER

God, You are all-knowing. You know our beginning and
our ending. You knew us when were shaped in our mothers'
wombs. Lord, only You know the direction that we need
to go. Teach us how to follow You, as You guide us through
life's journey. God, order our steps in your word and let
no sin rule over us. In the name of Jesus, I pray. Amen.

ENCOURAGEMENT

Who will/did you encourage today? How?

GRATITUDE

Identify three things that you are thankful for.

1.

2.

3.

ME-GIFTING

How will/did you treat yourself today?
Remember the rule: You cannot spend any money!

MY DAILY PROVERBS 31 DECLARATION

I am a virtuous woman, and my worth is far above that of rubies. I will do good and not evil all the days of my life. I will extend my hand to those in need. I am clothed with strength and dignity. I will speak words of wisdom and kindness. I will fear the Lord and my deeds will speak for me.

PROVERBS 31:10, 12, 20, 25, 26, 30, AND 31

Day 34

WHAT DID YOU JUST SAY?!!

DIONDRA MCFARLAND

*Do not let unwholesome [foul, profane, worthless, vulgar] words
ever come out of your mouth, but only such speech as is good for
building up others, according to the need and the occasion, so
that it will be a blessing to those who hear [you speak].*

EPHESIANS 4:29 AMP

I love watching reality television. My favorite is the Real Housewives series. Whenever I'm watching it, my husband walks out of the room and says, "I don't know why you're watching that mess!" One particular evening I was watching an episode and there was an argument between two ladies that was so vulgar my mouthed dropped open. I couldn't believe what was coming out of one woman's mouth on national television. My husband walked back in our room and said, "What did she just say?!!"

Recently, I was reading one of my Facebook memories that I shared last year from renowned motivational speaker Les Brown. His words are so befitting for this lesson:

> "Avoid foul-mouthed people. If you're one of them commit to lose this part of yourself. Don't allow yourself to be a vessel or a sponge for filthy or disrespectful language, or a garbage disposal for violent words—especially from people who are supposed to love you."

Are your words edifying in situations that try your patience? The slow cashier in the grocery store. The driver that cut you off. Dealing with the disobedient child. For many of us, "nice" words are not always the first words. I love *The Message* translation of Proverbs 18:21:

> "Words kill, words give life; they're either poison or fruit—you choose."

One of the biggest lies that we were taught as children was, "Sticks and stones may break my bones but words will never hurt me." Bones mend but words cut like a knife and kill. A woman of strength and dignity should temper her words and is mindful of how she communicates, especially in hostile situations. Proverbs 16:24 (NLT) says, "Kind words are like honey—sweet to the soul and healthy for the body."

> A careful word may kindle strife
>
> A cruel word may wreck a life
>
> A bitter word may hate instill
>
> A brutal word may smite or kill
>
> A gracious word may smooth the way
>
> A joyous word may lighten the day
>
> A timely word may lessen stress
>
> A loving word may heal and bless. (Author Unknown)

Remember, my dear sister, words matter. Don't allow them to compromise your witness. Pray Psalm 19:14 (KJV), "Let the words of my mouth, and the meditation of my heart, be acceptable in thy sight, O LORD, my strength and my redeemer."

THOUGHT FOR TODAY

Cursing is the strongest expression of a weak mind. Use words that represent the highest and best expression of yourself, and of what you see for your future and your life. You deserve it!

LES BROWN

SCRIPTURE READING

Proverbs 15:1

Proverbs 18:21

Galatians 5:22–23

2 Peter 1:5–6

REFLECT

1. What triggers you to use foul language?

2. Read Philippians 4:8. Why is it important to concentrate on pure thoughts?

3. What steps will you make to speak in honorable ways?

TODAY'S PROMISE: PROTECTION

Even though I walk through the darkest valley, I will fear no evil, for you are with me; your rod and your staff, they comfort me.

PSALM 23:4 NIV

PRAYER

Create in me a clean heart, O God, and renew within me a right spirit. Father, I acknowledge that my words and thoughts matter. I choose to speak life and only those things that edify, uplift, and give You glory. Amen.

ENCOURAGEMENT

Who will/did you encourage today? How?

GRATITUDE

Identify three things that you are thankful for.

1.

2.

3.

ME-GIFTING

How will/did you treat yourself today?

Remember the rule: You cannot spend any money!

MY DAILY PROVERBS 31 DECLARATION

I am a virtuous woman, and my worth is far above that of rubies. I will do good and not evil all the days of my life. I will extend my hand to those in need. I am clothed with strength and dignity. I will speak words of wisdom and kindness. I will fear the Lord and my deeds will speak for me.

Proverbs 31:10, 12, 20, 25, 26, 30, and 31

Day 35

LEVEL UP! REACHING YOUR GOD-GIVEN POTENTIAL

JACQUELYN BAILEY WILLIAMS

*I tell you the truth, anyone who believes in me will
do the same works I have done, and even greater
works, because I am going to be with the Father.*

JOHN 14:12 NLT

One day my students and I discussed the word "potential." I asked them to think of something that started off differently than it ends up. I got so many different responses: (1) An egg has the potential to become a bird; (2) A lump of coal, after much pressure, can become a diamond; and (3) A caterpillar can become a butterfly. I told them to think about the idea that it is not where we start, it is how we finish that matters.

As women, we can all "level up" in God by growing in the knowledge of who He is and what He wants for your life—reaching your God-given potential!

Possibilities

As you look at the story of the Samaritan woman, this is a story of potential realized. As the story unfolds, this woman arrives at Jacob's well around noon. Why noon? Because according to the cultural and historical traditions of that time, women used to draw water in groups in the morning and it was often a social occasion. This woman had been married five times and was currently living with her boyfriend. These circumstances point to her desire to avoid the embarrassment that would come from attending the well when other women were present. However, this would be the day her life would change forever.

This woman, who was a sinner and a social outcast, lived in a world of guilt and loneliness. Suddenly, she found herself in Jesus' presence. He saw within her the potential to do a great work. Through all her experiences in life, Jesus showed her that having faith and simply attempting the "impossible" is life changing. When the woman believed, it propelled her into action, and she immediately ran off to tell her community and invite them to join her on the journey.

Have you ever felt that you must get past all your fears, faults, failures, and frailties before God can use you?

How You Can Level Up?

If we think about it, each one of us has potential, no matter how much we may have achieved already, and no matter how old we are. There's still more God has for each of us to be and do! But we must remember that no one can reach their potential without God's help. Only God knows the limits of our potential. All of us are finite and do not have the ability to fathom all that God has purposed for us.

The next time you are faced with an impossible situation, remember that God will provide a way. Each day he will give you a multitude of opportunities to reach the potential that God has placed within you.

THOUGHT FOR TODAY

The strength of a woman is not measured by the impact that all her hardships in life have had on her; but the strength of a woman is measured by the extent of her refusal to allow those hardships to dictate her and who she becomes.

C. JOYBELL

SCRIPTURE READING

Luke 2:52

1 Timothy 4:15

Ephesians 3:20

REFLECT

1. What is one excuse I am ready to stop using this year?

2. What is the step that I need to take today?

3. How can I bring God even more glory?

TODAY'S PROMISE: SAFETY

The LORD is my light and my salvation—whom shall I fear? The LORD is the stronghold of my life—of whom shall I be afraid?

PSALM 27:1 NIV

PRAYER

Father God, our potential, like our lives, is pointed toward You. We only exist to give You glory. And we can't achieve that potential without knowing You. You know the plans You have for us, plans for good and not for evil, to give us a future and a hope. Amen.

ENCOURAGEMENT

Who will/did you encourage today? How?

GRATITUDE

Identify three things that you are thankful for.

1.

2.

3.

ME-GIFTING

How will/did you treat yourself today?

Remember the rule: You cannot spend any money!

MY DAILY PROVERBS 31 DECLARATION

I am a virtuous woman, and my worth is far above that of rubies. I will do good and not evil all the days of my life. I will extend my hand to those in need. I am clothed with strength and dignity. I will speak words of wisdom and kindness. I will fear the Lord and my deeds will speak for me.

PROVERBS 31:10, 12, 20, 25, 26, 30, AND 31

COMING INTO YOUR ROYAL POSITION

SHAMEKA DIXON

For if you keep silent at this time, relief and deliverance
will rise for the Jews from another place, but you and your
father's house will perish. And who knows whether you
have not come to the Kingdom for such a time as this?

ESTHER 4:14 ESV

Some days you push full steam ahead, moving confidently toward
purpose. Other days you may wonder if what you are doing has
meaning. Persistence is the key to purpose.

Esther was an orphan. After the death of her parents, Mordecai (her
cousin) raised her as his own daughter. Esther was crowned queen and
was strategically placed in the king's palace to save the Jews.

Mordecai's encouragement to Esther to visit the king on behalf of
her people could have cost her her life. Going in the inner court without being called by the king was punishable by death. As her story
begins to unfold in the second chapter of Esther, we see how God was
very purposeful in everything Esther experienced. Esther's bravery led
to the freedom of her people. Esther could have very easily allowed fear
to lead her down a different path. Somewhere along the way she realized she was destined "for such a time as this."

Our lives can feel much like Esther's. There are some experiences we
face that seem unfair and unbearable. Yet, even in that God has a divine

purpose for every encounter, good or bad. God wastes nothing. Our lives have meaning and purpose. God told Jeremiah, "Before I shaped you in the womb, I knew all about you. Before you saw the light of day, I had holy plans for you: A prophet to the nations—that's what I had in mind for you" (Jeremiah 1:5 MSG).

God has something in mind for all His children.

There is no person—not a single man or woman—on earth by happenstance. Knowing God helps us to know who we are and why we are here. This is a realization the enemy tries desperately to keep us from. A woman living out her purpose is a force to be reckoned with. There will be opposition, but finding and living on purpose is so worth it.

We don't know the details of how Esther became an orphan. However, many women have experienced trauma and other life-altering events. People have spoken death over our hopes and dreams. At times we may have even believed our circumstances would stop God's purpose. Our own fears can hold us back as well. Esther continued in her purpose, saying, "If I perish, I perish" (Esther 4:16). God sometimes puts us in places of prominence to fulfill a purpose bigger than ourselves.

Everything God has for you is connected to walking in your purpose. We may not all be destined to be royalty like Queen Esther, but all of us can walk together in the purpose of bringing glory to God's name.

Please know that no amount of abuse, trauma, or opposition can deter us from God's purpose. Everything we think is unfavorable is usable by God. Keep praying. Keep showing up. Keep living on purpose.

THOUGHTS FOR TODAY

The moment anyone tries to demean or degrade you in any way, you have to know how great you are. Nobody would bother to beat you down if you were not a threat.

CICELY TYSON

You can't be hesitant about who you are.

VIOLA DAVIS

SCRIPTURE READING

Romans 8:28

1 Corinthians 10:31

Proverbs 19:21

REFLECT

1. What may be holding you back from walking in your divine purpose?

2. Have you identified your purpose?

3. What were you passionate about as a child?

4. Are you able to identify the people God placed in your life as "purpose pushers"?

TODAY'S PROMISE: LIGHT

But you are a chosen race, a royal priesthood, a holy nation, a people for his own possession, that you may proclaim the excellencies of him who called you out of darkness into his marvelous light.

1 PETER 2:9 NIV

PRAYER

Dear God, thank You for the woman reading this devotional.
Thank You for bringing her through every hardship and
struggle. Thank You that what tried to destroy her made
her stronger. Thank You for the unique and divine purpose
You placed in her. I ask that You guide her and protect
her as she walks boldly toward her purpose. Amen.

ENCOURAGEMENT

Who will/did you encourage today? How?

GRATITUDE

Identify three things that you are thankful for.

1.

2.

3.

ME-GIFTING

How will/did you treat yourself today?
Remember the rule: You cannot spend any money!

MY DAILY PROVERBS 31 DECLARATION

I am a virtuous woman, and my worth is far above that of rubies. I will do good and not evil all the days of my life. I will extend my hand to those in need. I am clothed with strength and dignity. I will speak words of wisdom and kindness. I will fear the Lord and my deeds will speak for me.

PROVERBS 31:10, 12, 20, 25, 26, 30, AND 31

MAMA NEEDS A MINUTE

MARGINA E. STAFFORD

Now standing beside Jesus' cross were his mother, his mother's
sister, Mary the wife of Clopas, and Mary Magdalene. So when
Jesus saw his mother and the disciple whom he loved standing
there, he said to his mother, "Woman, look, here is your son!"
He then said to his disciple, "Look, here is your mother!" From
that very time the disciple took her into his own home.

JOHN 19:25–27 NET

Have you ever hit the snooze button when your alarm sounded off in the morning? The snooze button is designed to silence the alarm for short intervals to allow time for more sleep. I am notorious for setting an alarm for a certain time in the morning, pressing the snooze button several times, and then not actually getting up until an hour later. I am *always* in need of a few more minutes of sleep. There are times when I wish there was a snooze button I could press and life as we know it would just pause for a moment, allowing me to catch up on some much-needed rest.

As women, we operate daily in several different capacities. As wives and mothers, we manage our homes. Some of us are employed or own a business. There are women who work in their community or in their local church. Some women are caretakers for loved ones. There are women who are students, pursuing higher education. Then there are those women who carefully balance a complex combination of several roles.

We often spend so much of our time pouring into the lives of others that we fail to take a minute to pour into ourselves. We work tirelessly to ensure that others are cared for and yet are many times guilty of denying others opportunities to care for us. Some of us tie our Superwoman capes on and spread ourselves so thin that our effectiveness to those we are serving suffers. As a result, we experience feelings of being overworked and overwhelmed.

A minute to rest, relax, recover, reset, refresh is really all we need. I was at clothing store and on display was a t-shirt that immediately caught my attention. "Mama needs a minute" were the words written across the front. As I eagerly found my size, I was overjoyed at the notion that someone else understood exactly how I felt!

As Mary, the mother of Jesus, stood by the cross, she witnessed her firstborn son experiencing a slow, agonizing, shameful death. As she watched her son dying from the sixth to the ninth hour, Mary was more than likely physically drained, emotionally distraught, mentally defeated and even spiritually distressed.

Jesus, while enduring His own excruciating suffering, discerned that to deal with how it weighed on her, His "Mama would need a minute." He commands that His mother be cared for, knowing that she would need some time to be comforted, to grieve, to process, and to rest. Jesus charges one of His closest disciples to look after His mother.

There are accounts in the Bible when Jesus Himself took moments to rest. Jesus said to His disciples "Let's go off by ourselves to a quiet place to rest awhile" (Mark 6:31 NLT). He said this because there were so many people coming and going that Jesus and His apostles didn't even have time to eat. Jesus, while divine in nature, displayed His humanity by demonstrating the need for physical rest.

So, take a minute, whatever that means for you, be it a day, week, or month. Take time to discover activities that help you get the rest you need. Release the feelings of guilt for taking time to care for yourself. If Jesus, while dying on the cross, paused to mandate that His mother take a minute, how much more should we routinely take a minute to care for ourselves, mind, body, and soul? In doing so, we will be more effective operating in the various capacities He has entrusted us to serve.

THOUGHTS FOR TODAY

*Rest time is not waste time. It is economy to gather fresh
strength. It is wisdom to take occasional furlough. In the
long run, we shall do more by sometimes doing less.*

CHARLES SPURGEON

*Wisdom is knowing when to have rest, when to
have activity, and how much of each to have.*

SRI SRI RAVI SHANKAR

When I'm tired, I rest. I say, "I can't be a superwoman today."

JADA PINKETT SMITH

SCRIPTURE READING

Genesis 2:3

Psalm 4:8

Matthew 11:28–30

REFLECT

1. How much time (during the day, week, or month) do you
   devote to taking moments of rest?

2. How can you rearrange your schedule to prioritize time for
   yourself?

3. What activities are most effective in renewing and
   refreshing your mind, body, and soul?

TODAY'S PROMISE: PARDON

*You, Lord, are forgiving and good, abounding
in love to all who call to you.*

PSALM 86:5 NIV

PRAYER

Heavenly Father, thank You for allowing me to understand
the importance of taking moments to rest. Help me to
prioritize these moments so that I can experience a better me
and so that I can better serve others in Your kingdom. Amen.

ENCOURAGEMENT

Who will/did you encourage today? How?

GRATITUDE

Identify three things that you are thankful for.

1.

2.

3.

ME-GIFTING

How will/did you treat yourself today?
Remember the rule: You cannot spend any money!

MY DAILY PROVERBS 31 DECLARATION

I am a virtuous woman, and my worth is far above that of rubies. I will do good and not evil all the days of my life. I will extend my hand to those in need. I am clothed with strength and dignity. I will speak words of wisdom and kindness. I will fear the Lord and my deeds will speak for me.

PROVERBS 31:10, 12, 20, 25, 26, 30, AND 31

Day 38

A WONDERFUL CHANGE

RAQUEL PIGEE

> *"If I just touch his clothes, I will be healed."*
> MARK 5:28 NIV

I know she didn't!" "Who does she think she is?" I can only imagine how this unnamed sister was viewed and talked about when she decided to step out in faith. She needed a change. So when she got the news that Jesus was in town, she made her way to get her breakthrough. She was not supposed to be in public since she was considered ceremonially unclean. But that wasn't going to hold her back. She desperately needed a change! She had faith that if she could encounter Jesus, she would be changed.

Let's step into her shoes. You have been hemorrhaging for twelve years. You have gone from doctor to doctor, yet there is no supplement, no medicine, no surgery, absolutely nothing that will stop the bleeding. To add insult to injury, you have run out of money to pursue any further help.

Yes! That's the landscape of what she was dealing with. She needed a change, so she pressed in through the crowd thinking, "If I just touch his clothes, I will be healed." Mark 5:29 (NIV) continues, "Immediately her bleeding stopped, and she felt in her body that she was freed from her suffering." And just like that, the season of her suffering was over. A wonderful change had taken place in her body.

Keep it real: Sometimes it seems like the rain will never stop.

Sometimes it seems like the storm will never end. The situation that you are dealing with was supposed to be over and done with, but here you are weeks, months, if not years later still in that struggle. Don't give up, my sister! Trouble won't last always. Take heart and hold on to your faith in God. He will take care of you!

Regardless of what we may encounter in this life or how long we have dealt with certain issues, please trust and believe that God. Is. In. Control. With just one touch from Jesus, we can experience a wonderful change that invigorates us. We will enjoy a fresh and beautiful new season in our lives.

Keep pushing forward, Sister! Don't turn around. Your wonderful change is just a touch away!

THOUGHT FOR TODAY

You are on the eve of a complete victory. You can't go wrong. The world is behind you.

JOSEPHINE BAKER

SCRIPTURE READING

Psalm 118:1

Jeremiah 29:11

Matthew 7:7–12

Mark 5:25–34

1 John 5:14–15

REFLECT

1. Do you feel like you desperately need a change, but are afraid to take the steps toward that change? What are some of the obstacles that you are facing?

2. List actions that you will need to take in order to evoke the change that you need in your life.

3. What changes have you trusted God for in the past and received a breakthrough? Explain them below and use this to encourage yourself in your present situation.

TODAY'S PROMISE: SECURITY

The LORD is a refuge for the oppressed, a stronghold in times of trouble. Those who know your name trust in you, for you, LORD, have never forsaken those who seek you.

PSALM 9:9-10 NIV

PRAYER

Father, we need a wonderful change to occur in our lives. Please give us the strength and courage to reach beyond our fears and anxieties to touch You. Help us to keep our eyes and hearts on You. Empower us with knowing that You will orchestrate the change that we need in our lives. Give us peace, joy, healing, purpose, and a walk of excellence. In Jesus' name we pray, amen.

ENCOURAGEMENT

Who will/did you encourage today? How?

GRATITUDE

Identify three things that you are thankful for.

1.

2.

3.

ME-GIFTING

How will/did you treat yourself today?

Remember the rule: You cannot spend any money!

MY DAILY PROVERBS 31 DECLARATION

I am a virtuous woman, and my worth is far above that of rubies. I will do good and not evil all the days of my life. I will extend my hand to those in need. I am clothed with strength and dignity. I will speak words of wisdom and kindness. I will fear the Lord and my deeds will speak for me.

PROVERBS 31:10, 12, 20, 25, 26, 30, AND 31

REDISCOVERING ME: GO GET THAT GIRL!

VICKIE BARBER-CARROLL

"Or suppose a woman has ten silver coins and loses one. Doesn't she light a lamp, sweep the house and search carefully until she finds it? And when she finds it, she calls her friends and neighbors together and says, 'Rejoice with me; I have found my lost coin.' In the same way, I tell you, there is rejoicing in the presence of the angels of God over one sinner who repents."

LUKE 15:8–10 NIV

We are overwhelmed and distracted with life. We have spouses, parents, children, partners, and the list continues. At times, we have to give ourselves permission to "do us." This is not selfish, it is necessary. In Luke 15, Jesus tells the parable of the woman looking for the lost coin. She had something of value, and it was lost.

This parable helped me realize that, with all my day-to-day activities, I had become distracted. I go to work, pick up the kids, go to the store, cook dinner, go over homework, clean up the kitchen—oh yes, and then I spend time with my mate.

Guess what? I have spent zero minutes on myself. When I do take a few minutes to stop and think, I realize that I have some personal goals that I desire to fulfill, but they have been pushed aside. We are always supporting everyone in their ventures. We often have goals, dreams, and aspirations that remain unfulfilled. In this parable, the woman loses one of her coins and she doesn't stop looking until she finds it. It became evident to me that I was the woman in the parable that had become distracted, and the coin was representative of my personal goals and dreams.

Proverbs 31:10 reminds us of how valuable we are not just to others but to ourselves. We have to challenge and search ourselves to find those God-given talents that are within us. We get so buried and burned out over everyone else's stuff. Let's face it, sometimes we feel the need to take care of everybody and their problems. We must find the courage and time to look within ourselves and birth that business you wanted to start, that project that was never finished, that degree that you started or wanted to achieve, and the list continues.

I want to encourage you to take a day, a weekend, or even a few hours and think about something you've enjoyed or left undone. Block out all distractions. Of course, I know how we do it. We think of things or times when we've had fun with the kids or our mates. That's not what I mean. I'm talking about a time when you've read a book, gone swimming, taken a long bath, taken a class, walked the trail, slept in, etc.

As we get older, we often forget to carve out a minute for ourselves. We have to go get that girl within us that wants to soar. I want to encourage you to find a few minutes, hours, or days to "do you" with no guilt. Search your thoughts and heart as intently as the woman in the parable looking for the lost coin. Give yourself permission to live. Reset your goals and do some of the things that you enjoy and that God has called you to do. Rediscover yourself and go get that girl that dared to dream!

THOUGHT FOR TODAY

If you prioritize yourself, you are going to save yourself.
GABRIELLE UNION

SCRIPTURE READING

Psalm 37:23–24

Philippians 4:13

Luke 6:31

REFLECT

1. What steps can you take to live your best life?

2. What can you do to set aside more time for yourself and God?

3. How can you display the persistence of the woman in the parable in your everyday life?

TODAY'S PROMISE: REDEMPTION

If you declare with your mouth, "Jesus is Lord," and believe in your heart that God raised him from the dead, you will be saved.

ROMANS 10:9 NIV

PRAYER

Oh God! Lead and guide me as I seek to rediscover the value and purpose that You have for my life. Amen.

ENCOURAGEMENT

Who will/did you encourage today? How?

GRATITUDE

Identify three things that you are thankful for.

1.

2.

3.

ME-GIFTING

How will/did you treat yourself today?

Remember the rule: You cannot spend any money!

MY DAILY PROVERBS 31 DECLARATION

I am a virtuous woman, and my worth is far above that of rubies. I will do good and not evil all the days of my life. I will extend my hand to those in need. I am clothed with strength and dignity. I will speak words of wisdom and kindness. I will fear the Lord and my deeds will speak for me.

PROVERBS 31:10, 12, 20, 25, 26, 30, AND 31

Day 40

STAYING THE COURSE

JULIE BERRY

Have I not commanded you? Be strong and courageous.
Do not be frightened, and do not be dismayed, for
the LORD your God is with you wherever you go.

JOSHUA 1:9 ESV

Women experience many obstacles that can pull us away from the path the Lord has ordained for us. Advancing a career, raising healthy children, tending to aging parents, and being a helpmate, among other tasks, can pull our focus away from what really matters. However, if we look for guidance from those who have already walked this route, we can be encouraged by their testimony and prepared for the journey.

The Bible illustrates bold and fearless women. Numbers 27:1–7 tells us about Zelophehad's five daughters (Mahlah, Noah, Hoglah, Milkah, and Tirzha) who went to Moses to plead for their father's inheritance, since he'd died with no male offspring to receive his property. *They got what they asked for!* Women are also portrayed as overcomers. In the first chapter of Ruth, she was able to move beyond a difficult past. Although Ruth grew up in a pagan society and worshipped idols, she accepted Naomi's God. Before meeting Boaz, she experienced the death of her first husband.

In addition, women served as mentors. Acts 18:24–28 tells the story of Priscilla and her husband Aquila; they worked well together not only as tentmakers, but as students of the Word. They invited Apollos into their home; they didn't criticize him, but they taught him. They shared their understanding of the Word with him, helping him to be a better proclaimer of it. Finally, a woman was the first to see Jesus after His resurrection. John 20:1–18 says Jesus revealed Himself to Mary Magdalene.

Although there are many other women in the Bible who fit this mold, when we consider these women, we see there are common trends. These women kept God first. God was a priority for each of them. Regardless of what each had going on in her life, they did not put God on that small burner on the stove. The four examples show that each woman had adversity to overcome. Perseverance was necessary to be an overcomer. Just when we feel like we've come to the end of our rope, we need to just hang on a little while longer. Additionally, each of the women had the right support system. Partnerships are vital. We should ALL have people in our corner to hold us accountable, to encourage us, and to pray with and for us.

They all had a positive impact on those around them. Wouldn't it make all the difference if all women were willing to pour into someone, speak life over someone, or mentor someone? After all, we are much better together.

God has given us the formula, the blueprint. If it worked for them and God honored and blessed them, then surely God will smile on us too.

If we take these four principles (make God a priority, persevere, develop healthy partnerships, and have a positive impact on those around you) and apply them to our own lives, we too can walk in victory.

Just as the Lord chose to use these powerful women in the Bible, you too can be used.

THOUGHT FOR TODAY

There's always something to suggest that you'll never be who you wanted to be. Your choice is to take it or keep on moving.

PHYLICIA RASHAD

SCRIPTURE READING

Proverbs 31:25

2 Timothy 1:5

2 Timothy 3:14–17

REFLECT

1. How can you exemplify godly character?

2. Who are some of the women in the Bible that you would like to model your life after?

3. How can you encourage other women to study the women of the Bible?

TODAY'S PROMISE: HEALING

Is anyone among you sick? Let them call the elders of the church to pray over them and anoint them with oil in the name of the Lord. And the prayer offered in faith will make the sick person well; the Lord will raise them up. If they have sinned, they will be forgiven.

James 5:14-15 NIV

PRAYER

Lord, help me to be the woman that You would have me to be according to Your word and will. Amen.

ENCOURAGEMENT

Who will/did you encourage today? How?

GRATITUDE

Identify three things that you are thankful for.

1.

2.

3.

ME-GIFTING

How will/did you treat yourself today?

Remember the rule: You cannot spend any money!

MY DAILY PROVERBS 31 DECLARATION

I am a virtuous woman, and my worth is far above that of rubies. I will do good and not evil all the days of my life. I will extend my hand to those in need. I am clothed with strength and dignity. I will speak words of wisdom and kindness. I will fear the Lord and my deeds will speak for me.

PROVERBS 31:10, 12, 20, 25, 26, 30, AND 31

Contributing Authors

Vickie Barber-Carroll, a native of Atlanta, is married to Bruce. They parent four children and currently serve both the Antioch and Shady Grove #2 Baptist Churches in Shreveport, Louisiana. Vickie is a career educator and administrator.

Alvester Williams Barfield and her husband, Irving, serve at Fairview Baptist Church in Elm Grove, Louisiana. They have four children and six grandchildren. Alvester has been an educator for forty-two years and loves reading, traveling, shopping, and working in the yard.

Julie Berry is the wife of Emory and the mother of two children. She is an educator, having earned a Doctor of Education at Virginia State University. She enjoys singing, cooking, reading, traveling, and mentoring young ladies. She and her husband have served congregations in three states.

Yulanda Blackshire studied at Bossier Parish Community College. She and her husband, Stanley, serve at Friendship Baptist Church in Grand Cane, Louisiana. Together they have four children, three grandchildren, and one great grandson. She enjoys her family and exercising.

Tomiko Fuller Cain is a preschool teacher and a graduate of Wiley College. She and her husband, Larry, serve at Saint John Baptist Church in Bellevue, Louisiana. Together they are parents to two daughters and one son and grandparents to three.

Taneca Dennis and her husband, Patrick, serve at Bright Star Baptist Church in Shreveport, Louisiana. They have a blended family of eight children and three grandchildren. She is a graduate of Wiley College.

Shameka Dixon and her husband, Antonio, have three children and a dog. Shameka is a mental health advocate and is currently pursuing a master's degree in counseling. The Dixons serve at Steeple Chase Baptist Church in Shreveport, Louisiana.

Nicole Eason and her husband, Tommy, serve at East Point Mount Zion Baptist Church in Coushatta, Louisiana. They have four children and one grandson. Nicole is a veteran and currently works as a human resources manager. She is a graduate of Bossier Parish Community College.

Judy Greer serves with her husband, Samuel, at Queen Esther Baptist Church in Muskegon Heights, Michigan. She is the mother of four biological children and three adopted children. A graduate of Jackson State University, Judy is a retired educator.

Beverly H. Houston lives in Shreveport, Louisiana. She and her husband, Francis, were blessed with six children and twenty-four grandchildren. She is a graduate of Mississippi Valley State University and a retired educator. She and her husband serve at Saint Paul Baptist Church.

Tiffany Jarrett lives in Tulsa, Oklahoma, with her husband, Sean, their five children, and one dog. A sports mom, businesswoman, and graduate of the University of Arkansas, Tiffany loves serving her church (New Jerusalem) and her family.

Sherbrina T. Jones is a graduate of Southern University. She is a certified life coach and a registered nurse. Sherbrina and her husband, Timothy, serve at Peaceful Rest Missionary Baptist Church in Shreveport, Louisiana. They are parents of three children.

Angela Lacey is the wife of Brandon and the mother of three. She and her husband serve at New Life Full Gospel House of Worship in Shreveport, Louisiana. Angela enjoys spending time with her family attending football games and ballets at the theater.

Maryanne Maiden is married to Duan. They have three children and two grandchildren. The Maidens serve at The Church of the Loving God in Dallas, Texas. Maryanne loves traveling and dating her husband.

Diondra McFarland and her husband, Theodore, serve at Unity Fellowship Missionary Baptist Church in Chicago. They have four adult children. Diondra loves event planning and interior design. She a lifelong learner.

Monica Blake Mickle is the wife of Collier. They serve at the Greater St. Mary Baptist Church in Shreveport, Louisiana. They are the parents of five children and two beautiful granddaughters. A graduate of LSU-Shreveport, Monica is a member of Alpha Kappa Alpha Sorority, Inc.

Raquel Pigee loves quality time with her husband, Manuel, and their two beautiful daughters. They serve at United Believers Baptist Church in Baton Rouge, Louisiana. Inspired by helping others, Raquel is a school district leader and Sunday school teacher.

Betty Cooper Rose is a native of Bossier City, Louisiana. She and her husband, Reginald, serve at Community Fellowship Missionary Baptist Church in Houston, Texas. They have three adult children and five grandchildren. Betty studies at Bossier Parish Community College.

Crystal Rose and her husband, Reginald, have two children. They serve at Mt. Paran Missionary Baptist Church in Texas City, Texas. She has been a flight attendant for over fifteen years and considers herself a lifelong student.

Sundrell Farley Rose is the mother of two, with twelve grandchildren and five great grandchildren. She holds a Bachelor of Christian Education and serves with her husband, Richard, at the Holy Trinity Missionary Baptist Church in Houston, Texas.

Nikisha Dotson Smith is married to Alejandro. They have two adult sons and one granddaughter. Nikisha is a licensed Realtor and an administrator for the Louisiana Department of Veterans Affairs. They serve at Light Hill Baptist Church in Shreveport, Louisiana.

Theresa Smith and her husband, Melvin, serve at Saint Mark Baptist Church in Doyline, Louisiana. They are the parents of four children and the grandparents of eight. Teresa enjoys reading, traveling, and family gatherings.

T. Nichole Spies is a counselor and licensed Marriage and Family Therapist. She holds a PhD in Christian Ministry and is CEO of H.O.P.E. Family Outreach. T. Nichole serves with her husband, JWT, at New Galilean Baptist Church in Jackson, Mississippi. She is the mother of three and the grandmother of three.

Margina E. Stafford is married to Kevin and they serve at Fellowship Baptist Church in Fresno, California. Together they have a blended family of seven children. A graduate of the University of Phoenix, she holds a Master of Science in Marriage, Family, and Child Therapy.

Lois Thomas and her husband, Roy, serve at Saint James Baptist Church in Shreveport, Louisiana. They have been married for more than fifty years and were blessed with three sons, a daughter, and eight grandchildren. Lois is retired and enjoys singing.

Anna Rideau-Trammell and her husband, Terrance, serve at The Light Christian Church in Greenwood, Louisiana. They have a blended family of five children and two grandchildren. Anna is a graduate of Greenwood Acres Bible College and author of *The Power of Prayer*.

Barbara Vaught serves with her husband, Marvin, at Galilee Baptist Church in Haughton, Louisiana. They have three children, three grandchildren, and two great grandchildren. A federal employee of thirty years, she enjoys cooking, canning, decorating, and reading.

Virgie J. Washington and her husband, Cartrie, serve at Bright Star Baptist Church (Queensborough) in Shreveport, Louisiana. They have five children, fourteen grandchildren, and two great grands. Virgie attended UCLA. She is an avid tennis fan and loves assimilating new members into the church.

Renee M. White (1975–2022) was married to Claude for eighteen years and was the mother of three. She served with her husband at Grace Baptist Church in Peoria, Illinois. Renee graduated from John Marshall Law School in Chicago.

Tiffany White earned an MBA from the University of New Orleans and serves as a resource development manager. She is passionate about financial wellness and supporting people with special needs. She and her husband, Maurice, have two children and serve at Zion Traveler Baptist Church in Ruston, Louisiana.

Jacquelyn Bailey Williams is the wife of Trent and mother of two sons. She received a Master's in Educational Administration from Tuskegee University. She serves with her husband at Miracle Missionary Baptist Church in Alexander City, Alabama.

Made in the USA
Monee, IL
19 April 2022

95036312R00118